CONVERGENCE OF SCIENCE AND SOCIETY

PANDEMIC 2020

CONVERGENCE OF SCIENCE AND SOCIETY

PANDEMIC 2020

Swarup K. Chakrabarti

KNOWLEDGE WORLD
KW Publishers Pvt Ltd
New Delhi

Bandhan
IGNITING POTENTIAL

ISBN 978-93-91490-29-4 Paperback

Published in India by Kalpana Shukla

KNOWLEDGE WORLD

KW Publishers Pvt Ltd
4676/21, First Floor, Ansari Road
Daryaganj, New Delhi 110002
Phone: +91 11 43528107
Marketing: kw@kwpub.in
Editorial: production@kwpub.in
Website: www.kwpub.in

Printed and Bound in India

Contents

Part Two: The Multifaceted Societal Impact of COVID-19 on Science & Technology, and Innovation: Indian and Global Perspective

Preface

This volume marks the second major publication of the vertical on 'Science and Society in India: Issues of Convergence', attached to H.P. Ghosh Research Centre, the research wing of Bandhan-Konnagar, India. As we approach the second anniversary of COVID-19 pandemic around the world, the virus has killed about 5.5 million people worldwide, and resulted in an economic loss of about US$ 4 trillion, making it the largest global disrupt or since World War II. A return to the normalcy of pre-pandemic life remains an elusive dream. However, the unprecedented advancement of science, technology, and innovation (STI) has enabled the global society to effectively respond to the pandemic in medical terms and take gradual steps to address the issue of economic loss and move towards a sustainable bright future, amidst the never-ending COVID-19 pandemic.

In this context the present book has sought to capture India's experience with vaccine development and mass vaccination programme. I am sure the research findings incorporated in the volume will contribute to a better understanding of how India's COVID-19 management strategy can be further improved to serve the healthcare system and meet other key societal needs, especially of the marginalized communities, who have become the worst victims of the pandemic. Such understanding is crucial for enriching the discourses on sustainable development of the Indian society from a long-term perspective.

I complement Dr. Swarup K. Chakrabarti, the Research Analyst of H.P. Ghosh Research Centre, for producing this competent study.

I also thank Professor Dhrubajyoti Chattopadhyay, the eminent microbiologist/virologist and currently the Hon'ble Vice-Chancellor of Sister Nivedita University, Kolkata, for providing the necessary guidance in completing the research project. H.P. Ghosh Research Centre looks forward to supporting such socially relevant studies, as the present one. I also congratulate KW Publishers for publishing the book in a remarkably short time.

Chandra Shekhar Ghosh
Founder, Bandhan Bank

Introduction

> "This pandemic has magnified every existing inequality in our society-like systemic racism, gender inequality, and poverty."
>
> – Melinda Gates

> "Science and technology are going to be the basis for many of the solutions to social problems."
>
> – Frances Arnold

Since the beginning of the ongoing pandemic, COVID-19 has been reshaping science & technology (ST), innovation (I), impacting the society to a great extent. Factors that play key roles in shaping the future of ST, and innovation, such as intensity of research of development (R&D) across various sectors, and its disparity, the eagerness in adopting modern digital tools and technologies, the transparency, inclusiveness, and the spontaneity of advanced scientific research and innovation ecosystems, become more prominent in expanding benefits of STI uniformly across society.

The contribution of STI at this time of worst crisis, is not only key for encountering current health challenges, but, also, for supporting future production efforts, targeted at fast-paced economic recovery after the pandemic. In essence, the contributions of STI revolutionize four major key areas: first, R&D to understand the fundamental basis of a new infectious disease, its effects on the population, pharmacological intervention of the disease, that includes vaccines, and other medications; second, management of critical supplies and equipments, such as diagnostic tests, mechanical ventilators, and the development of advanced applications for tracking and prevention of the disease; third, economic recovery by developing digital platforms, for health, education, work from home or anywhere, and seamless technology transfer to the society for larger benefits and industrial reconversion.

Importantly, STI can effectively reduce a high socio-economic cost by improving healthcare performance, such as lowering the duration of hospitalization stay, and associated treatment cost in COVID-19 victims through vaccinations, and by eliminating and/or reducing the economic burden on the society, due to extensive lockdowns and related sanitary, and social distancing measures.

Moreover, one of the key components of social inequality that becomes distinctly visible, during a worldwide pandemic is health inequality that is dependent on the socioeconomic and cultural disparities in the population. Thus, one of the key aspects of the Sustainable Development Goals (SDGs) is the attainment of good health, and wellbeing (SDG3), in the general population. Also, social inequality leads to disparities in the distribution of health-related benefits, such as vaccine equity, and the quality of the healthcare.

Additionally, social inequality that causes health inequality in the population, results from the unequal distribution of the social capital: knowledge gain through personal, and community network, that is inherent in the individual or at the community level. Thus, social policies, that promote social capital building, along all sections of society, is beneficial for improved healthcare access, that in turn strengthens a society's response to any emerging pandemic, across the world. This will further help protecting people belong to all socioeconomic classes, from a deadly infectious disease, by preventing transmission of infections from the most vulnerable, and healthcare deprived section of the society.

Thus, program, such as universal vaccination, remove health inequalities through building social capital, by improving vaccine awareness, and knowledge in the population, and negating economic disparities, by providing free access of vaccination to the population, who may not be able to afford it, to establish vaccine equity.

A pandemic situation helps the society to better understand the consequence of socioeconomic and cultural disparities, that exist in the population, and the importance of vaccination, and other diagnostic and treatment modalities, in not only preventing the transmission of the infectious disease and its severity, but, also, introduces cohesion in the society, that is essential to working together towards other common goals, in the true spirit of SDGs.

Moreover, science policy, science diplomacy, science publications, bilateral, and multilateral cooperation in the STI sector have taken the center stage during the ongoing COVID-19 pandemic. The rapid advancements in these areas will benefit STI across the world, and their sustainment, that will further help in establishing a better normal compared to pre-pandemic normal, after the current pandemic ends, sooner or later. Thus, 'Science' and 'Science-Advice' became the important components, in the decision making process, to mitigate the worst consequences of a worldwide pandemic.

Taken together, the book entitled "Convergence of Science and Society: Pandemic 2020" covers the multiple aspects of STI's beneficial roles, in reshaping the lives of the humans, and the society, during the worst crisis from a global pandemic in the 21st century.

References

OECD: Tackling Coronavirus (COVID-19)- Contributing to a global effort. https://www.oecd.org/coronavirus.

Economic integration in Latinamerica: the theoretical vision of ECLAC against the evolution project in the region/integracion economica en America teoricade.

R. V. Lopez. *Journal of Economics, Finance and Administrative Science* 16 (31), 107-119, 2011.

From millennium development goals to sustainable development goals. J. D. Sachs. *The Lancet* 379 (9832), 2206-2211, 2012. DOI: https://doi.org/10.1016/S0140-6736(12)60685-0.

Social capital and public health: responding to the COVID-19 pandemic. A.S.Y. Wong and J.C. Kohler. *Global Health* 16, 88 (2020). DOI: https://doi.org/10.1186/s12992-020-00615-x).

Rethinking approaches of science, technology, and innovation in healthcare during the COVID-19 pandemic: the challenge of translating knowledge infrastructures to public needs. R. G. L. Da Silva, R. Chammas, H. M. D. Novaes. *Health Research Policy and Systems* 19 (1), 1-9, 2021. DOI: https://doi.org/10.1186/s12961-021-00760-8.

Science policy, science diplomacy, bilateral, and multilateral cooperation (https://www.indiascienceandtechnology.gov.in/bilateral-cooperations? category=department-of-biotechnology)

Science, society, and policy in the face of uncertainty: reflections on the debate around face coverings for the public during COVID-19. G.P. Martin, E. Hanna, M. McCartney, R. Dingwall. *Critical Public Health* 30 (5), 501-508, 2020. DOI: https://doi.org/10.1080/09581596.2020.1797997.

Offline: Independent science advice for COVID-19-at last. Richard Horton. *Lancet.* 2020 9-15 May, 395(10235): 1472. DOI: https://doi.org/10.1016/S0140-6736(20)31098-9.

PART ONE

The Tell Tale of Vaccination

The History of Vaccinations

"Vaccines are the tugboats of preventive health."

– William Foege

"If you want to know the value of vaccines, just spend some time in a clinic in Africa. The faces of mothers and fathers say it all: vaccines prevent illness and save lives."

– Seth Berkley

"In science credit goes to the man who convinces the world, not the man to whom the idea first occurs."

– Francis Galton

One of the major contributions of STI is the development of vaccines that save hundreds, and thousands of lives in the world. The practice of immunization dates back hundred of years. Historical evidence suggests that Buddhist monks used to drink snake venom to confer immunity to snakes bite. Also, evidence exists that the Chinese employed smallpox inoculation or variolation (smearing of a skin tear with cowpox to confer immunity to smallpox) in the 17th century. Also, it was practiced in Africa and Turkey, before it spreads to Europe, and the Americas.

Edward Jenner is considered the founder of vaccinology in the west. In 1796, he inoculated a 13-year-old-boy with vaccinia virus (cowpox), and was able to demonstrate immunity to smallpox. In 1798, the first smallpox vaccine was developed. However, Jenner's method underwent medical and technological changes over the next

200 years, and eventually resulted in the successful global eradication of smallpox, through systematic implementation of mass smallpox immunization.

In 1881, French biologist Louis Pasteur developed a successful vaccine against anthrax, in which, he exposed anthrax virus to heat and oxygen to weaken, but not to kill them. Additionally, in 1885, Pasteur developed vaccine against rabies. He used the same approach he did for the anthrax vaccine.

Furthermore, Louis Pasteur's experiments spearheaded the development of live attenuated cholera vaccine in 1897. The next routinely recommend vaccines were developed early in the 20th century. These included vaccines that protect against pertussis (1914), diphtheria (1926), and tetanus (1938). These three vaccines were combined in 1948, and given as DTP vaccine.

Importantly, the vaccine everyone was waiting for-the polio vaccine. Parents were scared of the polio epidemics that occurred each summer. In the absence of a polio vaccine, the only option for them was to keep their children away from the swimming pool, and sent them to stay with relatives in the country. All of them waited eagerly for an effective vaccine, and had been following the vaccine trial in the newspaper, and sending dimes to the White House, to assist the mission. In the end, polio vaccine was invented by Jonas Salk, and licensed in 1955. In 1963, the measles vaccine was developed, and by the late 1960s, vaccines were available to protect against mumps (1967) and rubella (1969). They combined into the MMR vaccine by Dr. Maurice in 1971.

Moreover, due to successful eradication efforts, the smallpox vaccine was no longer recommended for use after 1972. While vaccine research continued in full swing, new vaccines were not introduced during the 1970s. The vaccine for *Haemophilus influenzae* type B was licensed in 1985. The hepatitis B vaccine was licensed in 1981 and recommended for high-risk groups, such as infants, whose mothers were hepatitis B surface antigen positive, healthcare workers, intravenous drug users, homosexual men, and people with multiple sexual partners. However, this immunization strategy primarily targeted to priority groups, had failed to prevent completely the transmission of hepatitis B virus in the entire population, due to non-screening of hepatitis B virus in the non-high-risk groups. The change of recommendation to immunize all infants in 1991 was the results of these failed attempts, to control hepatitis B, by selectively immunizing high-risk groups. This approach seemed to work well, as hepatitis B disease was virtually eliminated in children less than 18 years of age, in the USA and in other parts of the world. Between 1995 and 2010, more vaccines were discovered and licensed; Varicella (chickenpox-1996), rotavirus (1998-1999; 2006, 2008), hepatitis A (2000); pneumococcal vaccine (2001). The schedule from 2011 to 2018 included meningococcal serogroup B vaccine (2014), additional recommendations for existing vaccines: HPV and intranasal influenza vaccine (2018), and discontinuation of intranasal influenza vaccine (2016). Lastly, the vaccines against SARS-CoV-2 (COVID-19) were developed in 2020, and many of them had received emergency use authorization (EUA) from the regulatory bodies across the world for mass vaccination, against COVID-19 disease in the individuals in 2021.

A brief history of vaccines and vaccinations in India

Smallpox was well known since ancient times, and believed to have originated in India or Egypt, over 3,000 years ago. One of the highest recorded smallpox epidemics was reported from Goa, India, in 1545 AD, when an estimated 8,000 children died. Many historians have sometimes referred smallpox as 'Indian Plague' that suggests the disease might be widely prevalent in India in the ancient times. The first dose of smallpox vaccine lymph in India arrived in May 1802. Anna Dusthell, a three-year-old child from Bombay (now Mumbai), became the first person in India to receive smallpox vaccine on June 14, 1802. In the initial period, lymph required for vaccination was primarily coming from Great Britain (now United Kingdom), and maintained in active state for further vaccination in Indian population.

In India, till 1850, the vaccine was imported from Great Britain. However, there were acute logistic challenges in the transportation of vaccine to India. The increased demand in later years led to the shortage of vaccine or lymph in the country, and had compelled Government of India to find alternatives for increasing sustained vaccine supply. There were incidents of few research efforts in Mumbai in 1832, and the animal experiment for the lymph started in Madras (now Chennai) in 1879, with initial success in 1880.

In the late 19th century, with increased vaccine production, the research focus had shifted to find a solution, for an effective preservation technique, to ensure transport of vaccines, to the rural and remote areas. In 1895, glycerine was used in India for efficient transport of vaccine material, in the form of glycerinated lymph paste. In addition, Lanoline and Vaseline were other preservatives, routinely used in India. Vaccine in boric acid formulation was also reported to be effective as vaccine preservative, developed in 1925.

Another critical event of this period was Cholera epidemic in Bengal, and in other parts of India. Following a recommendation of British Government, the Government of India approved cholera vaccine trial in India. In 1893, Dr. Haffkine, a representative from British Government, was assigned to conduct cholera vaccine trial in

India. He was able to show some efficacy of the cholera vaccine, in the effective management of the infectious disease.

However, as plague epidemic started in India in 1896, the Government of India advised Dr. Haffkine to work on the development of plague vaccine, and provided him space in Grant Medical College, Mumbai (now Haffkine Institute), to establish his laboratory. He successfully developed plague vaccine in 1897, and it is considered as the first vaccine developed in India.

The First World War (1914-1918) started and with coinciding Influenza pandemic that reportedly killed around 17 million Indians, and thus vaccination against influenza virus became a priority for the Government of India. Additionally, the new evidence emerged that two doses of smallpox vaccine would be needed for long-term protection from the disease. It was a major challenge for the government convincing people to get vaccinated twice with inconvenient, and painful vaccination procedures. The vaccination efforts continued with variable progress till 1939, when the World War II was started. As a result of the World War II, the nationwide vaccination coverage went down, and in 1944-1945, in India, the highest numbers of smallpox cases in the last two decades were reported. However, when the World War II ended, vaccination was ramped up again, and cases decreased suddenly.

At the time of independence, India had reported maximum numbers of smallpox cases in the world. Tuberculosis was also considered as a major cause of morbidity and mortality. In May 1948, the Government of India released a statement stating that tuberculosis was "assuming epidemic proportions" in the nation, and that "after careful consideration", agreed to introduce BCG (bacille Calmette-Guerin) vaccination against tuberculosis on a limited scale, and under strict supervision to control the disease. In August 1948, the first BCG vaccinations were conducted in India. In 1949, the BCG vaccination was further extended to schools in almost all States of India. The International Tuberculosis Campaign (ITC) supported government's effort to eliminating disease.

Furthermore, in 1988, the World Health Assembly passed a resolution for Polio eradication by 2000. Subsequently, Government of India joined global polio eradication efforts, and the first two National Immunization Days (NIDs) for poliomyelitis eradication in India were conducted on December 9, 1995 and January 20, 1996. An organized surveillance mechanism was initiated as National Polio Surveillance Project (NPSP) in 1997, through collaboration between the Government of India and the W.H.O (World Health Organization). Witnessing the success of disease eradication, on February 25, 2012, the W.H.O. had removed India from polio endemic countries.

In 2010, India became the last country in the world, to introduce second dose of measles vaccine in the NIP. The National Technical Advisory Group on Immunization (NTAGI) in India was constituted in 2001, and was reconstituted in 2010. Subsequently, India released the first National Vaccine Policy in 2011. The policy aims to provide guidelines for effective functioning, and implementation of immunization programs in India. The year 2012-2013 was declared as 'Year of intensification of Routine Immunization (IRI) in India. The objective was to improving coverage in selectively identified poor immunization-performing districts in India. The tasks included conducting more intense, regular reviews and monitoring and supervisions, improving cold chain status, and IEC (Institutional Ethics Committee) efforts for increasing coverage for all the antigens.

Furthermore, a new bivalent oral cholera vaccine, a meningitis-A vaccine, and an indigenous Japanese encephalitis (JE) vaccines were developed and manufactured by Indian vaccine makers, in collaboration with international partners, and subsequently licensed in India. Till 2012, the JE vaccine used for immunization in India was imported from outside country. In recent years, Department of Biotechnology (DBT), Department of Science and Technology (DST), Council for Scientific and Industrial Research (CSIR), Indian Council of Medical Research (ICMR), and few of their selected units (individual institutes), have started playing crucial, complementary and collaborative roles in vaccine research, and providing needful conceptual, and technological impetus, to the indigenous vaccine development.

Figure 1. The history of the timeline (column 1) emergence of infectious diseases, and the pathway towards development of vaccines (column 2) across the world

0910	Masters and Smallpox Described Separately
1000	Early Chinese Inoculation
1545	Smallpox Epidemic in India
1578	Whooping Cough Epidemic in Paris
1612	Typhoid Fever Strikes Royalty
1613	Spanish Epidemic
1625	Early Smallpox in North America
1633	Colonial Epidemic
1648	Quarantine in Boston
1661	Royal Support of Inoculation
1676	Sydenham Documents Measles Infection
1678	Early Medical Pamphlet of Smallpox
1679	The Indian Plague
1684	17th Century Smallpox Treatment

1699	Yellow Fever in the American Colonies
1706	Africa Use of Varioilation
1718	Variclation in Turkey
1721	Boston Smallpox Epidemic
1721	The First English Variclation
1735	The Plague Among Children
1740	Rubella: The "German Measles"
1749	Birth of Jenner
1751	London Smallpox Deaths
1767	Chickenpox: Disease Distinguished for Smallpox
1770	Protection by Cowpox Infection
1776	Smallpox Becomes a Weapon of War
1796	Jenner's Breakthrough
1813	US Vaccine Agency Established
1817	Cholera: The Pandemic Begin
1822	Birth of Pasteur
1841	Rubella: The Naming of the "Little Red"
1849	Cholera: Snow's Early Findings
1853	Mandatory Vaccination in UK
1861	Measles Plays a Role in the Civil War
1865	Disease of Silkworms
1877	Anthrax Investigations
1879	First Laboratory Vaccine
1881	Landmark Anthrax Vaccine Study
1882	Tuberculosis: Koch Isolates and Cultures Bacili
1884	Attenuating the Rabies Virus
1885	Another Success with Rabies Vaccine
1885	Cholera: Ferran's Vaccine
1885	Rables Vaccine Used in Humans
1893	Cholera: Haffidine's Indian Vaccine Trial
1894	First US Polio Epidemic

1899	Early Typhoid Vaccines Used by British Military
1905	North America Sees Last Yellow fever Epidemic
1906	Whooping Cough: Bacteria Isolated
1908	Polivirus Identified
1909	Air Dried Vaccine Developed in Paris
1911	Haffkine Develops Heat-Killed Cholera Vaccine
1916	New York City Polio Epidemic
1918	Influenza: Spanish Influenza Pandemic and Vaccines
1933	Influenza: Influenza Virus Isolated
1935	Early Polio Vaccine Trial
1936	Max Theiler Develops Yellow Fever Vaccine
1942	Hepatitis Outbreak Prompts Improved Vaccine Safety
1944	Vaccine for Japanese Encephalitis
1948	Koprowski Tests Polio Vaccine on Himself
1953	Salk Gives Vaccine to His Family
1954	Massive Polio Vaccine Trial Begins in US
1958	First Measles Vaccine is Tested
1960	Sabin's Polio Vaccine Licensed
1961	Cholera: Seventh Pandemic
1962	Attenuated Measles Vaccine Developed
1963	Measles Vaccine Licensed
1963	Rubeovax Licensed
1965	Testing of Mumps Vaccine
1967	Mumpsvax Licensed
1968	Vaccine for Hong Kong Influenza Pandemic
1969	Rubella Vaccine Licensed
1971	Rabies: New Inactivated Vaccine
1971	Measles, Mumps, Rubella Vaccine Licensed
1974	Tuberculosis: WHO Immunization Program
1976	Swine Influenza Vaccine
1977	Pneumococcal Vaccine Licensed

1979	Rubella: An Improved Vaccine is Licensed
1980	Smallpox Declared Eradicated
1981	Hepatitis B: First Submit Viral Vaccine in US
1986	Hepatitis B: Recombinant Vaccine Licensed
1987	Conjugate Hib Vaccine Licensed
1989	Oral Typhoid Vaccine Licensed in the US
1994	Polio Declared Eliminated from the Americas
1995	Hepatitis A: Vaccine Licensed
1995	Chickenpox Vaccine Licensed
2000	99% Reduction in Polio Cases
2002	Polio Eliminated in Europe
2006	HPV Vaccine Licensed in United States
2006	Rotavirus: Vaccine Recommended
2011	Measles in France, United States
2014	Group B Meningococcal Vaccine Approved
2014	West African Ebola Epidemic
2014	South-East Asia Region Polio-Free
2016	WHO Declares Zika Virus Emergency
2016	Type 2 Oral Polio Vaccine Discontinued
2017	Yemeni Cholera Epidemic
2018	Polio Eradication Update
2019	SARS-CoV-2 Pandemic
2020	COVID-19 Vaccines Developed

Figure 2. The timeline emergence of pandemics and the death toll associated with some of the worst pandemics.

Source: Center for Disease Control and Prevention (CDC, USA) et al.

References

Vaccine development; immunisation Advisory Centre. https://www.immune.org.nz/vaccines/vaccine-development

Edward Jenner and the history of smallpox and vaccination. S. Riedal. Proc (Bayl Univ Med Cent). 2005 Jan; 18(1): 21-25. DOI: https://doi.org/10.1080/08998280.2005.11928028.

History of Anthrax; Center for Disease Control and Prevention, USA. https://www.cdc.gov/anthrax/basics/anthrax-history.html.

Historical Perspectives A Centennial Celebration: Pasteur and the Modern Era of Immunization. https://www.cdc.gov/nmwr/preview/mmwrhtml/00000572.htm

Diphtheria Tetanus Pertusis (DTaP) Vaccine. S. A. Ogden, J.T. Ludlow, K. Alsayouri. [Updated 2021 Feb 16]. In: StatPearls [Internet]. Treasure Island (FL): StatPearls Publishing; 2021 Jan. https://www.ncbi.nlm.nih.gov/books/NBK545173/#_NBK545173_pubdet_

History of polio vaccination. A. Baicus. *World J Virol.* 2012 Aug 12; 1(4):108-114. DOI: https://doi.org/10.5501/wjv.v1.i4.108.

History of Measles, Center for Disease Control and Prevention, USA. https://www.cdc.gov/measles/about/history.html.

Seminars in Pediatric Infectious Disease. M. R. Hilleman. 16 (3): 225-226. July 2005. DOI: https://doi.org/10.1053/j.spid.2005.05.002

Hepatitis A and Hepatitis B; History of Vaccines. https://www.historyofvaccines.org/content/articles/hepatitis-and-hepatitis-b

Hib vaccine. https://en.m.wikipedia.org/wiki/Hib_vaccine

Chickenpox (Varicella); History of Vaccines. https://www.historyofvaccines.org/content/articles/chickenpox-varicella

Rotavirus Vaccines: a story of success with challenges ahead. M. 0'Ryan. Version 1. F1000Res. 2017; 6: 1517. DOI: https://doi.org/10.12688/f1000research.11912.1

A brief history of pneumococcal vaccines. R Austrian. Drugs Aging. 1999. DOI: https://doi.org/10.2165/00002512-199915001-00001

History of meningococcal vaccines and their serological correlates of protection. April 2012. C. Vipond et al. *Vaccine* 30 Suppl 2:B10-7. DOI: https://doi.org/10.1016/j.vaccine.2011.12.060

History and evolution of influenza control through vaccination: from the first monovalent vaccine to universal vaccine. I. BARBERIS, P. MYLES, S.K. AULT, N.L. BRAGAZZI, and M. MARTINI. *J Prev Med Hyg.* 2016 Sep; 57(3): E115-E120.

Coronavirus vaccine development : from SARS and MERS to COVID-19. Y.D. Li et al. *J Biomed Sci* 27, 104 (2020). DOI: https://doi.org/10.1186/s12929-020-00695-2

The Indian queens who modelled for the world's first vaccine. BBC News. https://www.bbc.com/news/world-asia-india-53944723

Haffkine in India; History of Vaccines. https://www.historyofvaccines.org/content/haffkine-India

BCG vaccination in India and tuberculosis in children: newer facets. P. M. Udani. Indian J Pediatr. Sep-Oct 1994; 61(5): 451-62. DOI: https://doi.org/10.1007/BF02751703

CDC and the Global Polio Eradication Initiative. https://www.cdc.gov/polio/who/index/htm

Polio in India-Polio Documentation India. https://iple.unicef.in/pages/polio-india-history.html

India's National Technical Advisory Group on Immunisation. T. J. John. DOI: https://doi.org/10.1016/j.vaccine.2010.02.041

Universal Immunization Program-Ministry of Health and Family. https://main.mohfw.gov.in

Development of a vaccine to prevent Japanese encephalitis: a brief review. V. Wiwanitkit. *Int J Gen Med.* 2009; 2: 195-200. DOI: https://doi.org/10.2147/jigm.s6281

The Induction of Immunity

> "The immune systems goals is to protect the body against invaders either from without, such as microbes, or from within, such as cancers and different types of neoplastic transformation."
>
> – Anthony S. Fauci

> "I like to read general biology-things about the immune system and advances in that area-because it lays the foundation for my part of the dialogue at the foundation about what things we ought to pursue."
>
> – Bill Gates

The immune system has evolved to protect the host from a multitude of pathogenic microbes. The host uses both cell-mediated innate and antibody-meditated adaptive mechanisms, to identify foreign pathogen, and elicit an effective immune response, against the invading pathogens and eliminate them. Both of these mechanisms depend on the hosts' inherent ability to discriminate self-antigens from non-self antigens. Unlike the innate immunity, that is non-specific in terms of detecting foreign antigens, the adaptive immune system is activated, through recognition of antigen-specific receptors, expressed on the surfaces of T- and B-lymphocytes.

Antibody production in the body

The detailed mechanisms of the immune response are beyond the scope of the current edition of the book, however, it is useful, to have an overview of how antibodies are produced by the immune system.

When our body encounters a foreign molecule (primarily protein) through natural infection or by vaccination, the immune responses are initiated. Vaccination has long been known to be an effective solution to preventing an infectious disease. In general, to produce a robust immune response, the initial first dose of vaccine, and couple of booster doses are given to an individual to produce adequate amount of antibodies that can protect the individual either for a limited time period or throughout the life depending on the nature of the vaccine, and the disease it aims to protect. Simplistically, the way it works is that once infection goes away using neutralizing antibodies, that block the attachment and entry of virus or any other pathogen to the host cells, the body is left with a supply of memory T- and B- lymphocytes, that remain dormant until the next time they encounter the same pathogen, to illicit a much faster and stronger immune response against any infection with the same pathogen or against any booster dose of the vaccine, used to protect the same infection.

Antibodies are made in the body, when we encounter naïve antigen first time, specialized immune cells, such as macrophages and dendritic cells that bridge between innate and adaptive immune systems, capture, and begin processing to present the antigens to B cell lymphocytes to produce antibodies. Antibodies obtain their diversity and quality by two processes. The first is called V (D) J (variable, diverse, and joining regions) recombination. Second, a fine-tuning occurs when B cells activation take place, where V domains of the H (heavy) and L (light) chains undergo high rate of point mutations, a process known as somatic hypermutation that gives diversity of the antibody pool which helps B cell lymphocytes to produce higher affinity antibodies outperforming lower affinity ones, through a process known as "affinity maturation". Each B cell lymphocyte produces one unique antibody against one unique epitope or antigenic determinant of the pathogen.

The duration of protective immunity after an infection

The duration of protective immune response varies with the nature of the pathogen. A study was done in China in 2007 on 176 patients developed severe acute respiratory syndrome (SARS). The SARS-specific antibodies were maintained for an average of two years, and significant reduction of immunoglobulin G (IgG) levels occurred in the third year. Thus, presumably, SARS patients might be susceptible to re-infection after three years of initial exposure. A new study entitled "Immunological Memory to SARS-CoV-2 Assessed for up to 8 Months after Infection" was published in the journal *Science*. The data suggest nearly all COVID-19 survivors have the desired immune cells necessary to fight re-infection for five to eight months or more.

Since the massive vaccination against SARS-CoV-2 has started in the beginning of 2021 worldwide, it will take more time to better understand the duration of the real-world immunity protection against COVID-19 disease. It is possible that when protective, neutralizing antibodies disappear from the blood stream, memory B cells lymphocytes, T helper cells (Th), and cytotoxic (killer) T cells remain in the blood stream to fight future re-infection. Indeed, lately, researchers in the La Jolla Institute (LJI) for Immunology in San Diego, California, USA, has analyzed blood samples from 188 COVID-19 patients. Among 7 per cent of them who are hospitalized, they measured not only virus-specific antibodies in the blood stream, but also memory B- and T- cells (Th), and cytotoxic T cells. The data suggest that immune memory persists in at least all three immunological compartments in about 95 per cent of subjects five to eight months post-symptom onset, implying that durable immunity against secondary COVID-19 disease is possible in most infected individuals.

A key question is whether COVID-19 vaccinations provide the similar level and duration of immune protection, against the disease observed in active infections, has yet to be determined with certainty, in the absence of a long-term follow up on previously infected patients, but indications are protection may be equally strong.

New evidence shows that even though fully vaccinated people remain at risk for SARS-CoV-2 infections, they are substantially less prone to carry infection compared to unvaccinated ones. A point-prevalence survey of about 100,000 people conducted in England in June-July 2021 during the surge of COVID-19 Delta variant found that fully vaccinated people (n=55962) were two-third less likely to carry SARS-CoV-2 compared with unvaccinated people (n=15135), with absolute rates of 0.40% versus 1.21%, respectively. Additionally, in a randomized trial of the mRNA-1273 vaccine (Moderna) versus placebo, vaccinated participants (n=14,287) were two-third less likely to be asymptotic carriers compared to unvaccinated participants (n=14,161), with absolute rates of 1.5% versus 3.5%, respectively.

Does drop in the level of antibodies result in loss of protective immunity against a pathogen?

At present, based on the accumulating data on recent COVID-19 infected cases, there is no consensus, and understanding on the safe levels of neutralizing antibodies, and how long is the protection lasts. Even if the antibodies do decrease over time that does not mean that the person is necessarily unprotected, since there may be memory T-cell responses, that are protective against re-infection from the same pathogen. However, we still do not know why for some vaccines protect for mere weeks against specific diseases, but other works for life to give us a long-lasting immunity.

Moreover, apart from developing a strong systemic immunological memory, the key is to develop neutralizing antibodies (nAbs), that block the entry of the pathogen, such as virus to the host cells, as opposed to simple antibodies, that bind specifically to the pathogen, but do not interfere with their infectivity. Thus, seroprevalance of a natural infection or vaccination does not always necessarily tell us the ability of an individual, to resist re-infections. Long lasting nAbs in larger amounts, might help to stay away from the re-infections, for a long period of time. The age of the individual, genetic and epigenetic make up, strength of the antigen presenting cells (APCs) are key determinants, for the production of effective nAbs. Furthermore, it also depends on the type of vaccination. A vaccination that releases the antigen/immuongen, over a long period of time, such as using replication-competent, engineered, viral vaccine delivery system, typically produces longer duration of immune protection, against an infectious disease.

T-cell vaccination

A T-cell vaccine is designed to induce protective T-cells, such as the CD4+ T helper cells and CD8+ cytotoxic T cells. It is observed that often it is difficult to develop antibodies against a specific pathogen in some individuals. It is possible that they may not have adequate numbers of functional T cells, that assist in the production of antibodies from B cell lymphocytes in the body. Furthermore, T cells are also essential to the induction of immune memory that saves us from further re-infection from the same pathogen, more effectively in the future. However, the truth is, there are hardly any T-cell therapeutics, for infectious diseases available, till date. Importantly, it has been shown that those with the most severe form of the disease, due to infection from SARS-CoV-2, have extremely low numbers of T cells lymphocyte. One of the clinical trials, listed in the ClinicalTrials.gov, will evaluate if a drug, interleukin 7, that is known to augment T-cell numbers can aid patients' recovery.

Do we need booster vaccine shots after getting fully vaccinated?
As per the W.H.O, as of now, it is still not clear whether or not a booster shot will be needed. The caveat is that since majority of the individuals in most parts of the world have not yet completed a first complete course of COVID-19 vaccination, it is too premature to come up with a verdict. However, according to a recent press release, by the biopharmaceutical company Pfizer, people will "likely" need a booster dose of COVID-19 vaccine, within 12 months of getting fully vaccinated. As per Johnson & Johnson, another biopharmaceutical company, people may need to get vaccinated against COVID-19 annually. According to Center for Disease Control and Prevention (CDC, USA), protection from some childhood vaccines can wear off over time. Thus many of the individuals may be at risk for vaccine-preventable disease due to age, nature of the job, lifestyle, travel, and health condition. For adults 19-26 years old, in addition to seasonal flu (influenza) vaccine and Td or Tdap vaccine (Tetanus, diphtheria, and pertussis), ideally one should also get human papillomaviruses vaccine (HPV) that protects against the types of human HPV that cause cervical, anal, and other cancers (CDC, USA). All adults need a seasonal flu vaccine and Td vaccine but there may be additional booster vaccine shots for people who have pre-existing conditions such as T1D (Type I Diabetes) and T2D (Type 2 Diabetes), CVDs (cardiovascular diseases), HIV

(Human Immunodeficiency Virus) infection, lung diseases, such as asthma, and renal disease.

Interestingly, the largest (n=1.5 million) third dose of study using Pfizer-BioNTech mRNA vaccine was conducted in Israel among individuals who received a third dose of vaccine between July 30, 2020 and September 23, 2021 and matched (1:1) to demographically and clinical similar controls who did not receive a third dose. The third dose and control groups consisted of 728.321 individuals each. The primary outcomes measured were hospital admission for COVID-19, severe COVID-19 disease, and COVID-19-related deaths. The data showed short-term vaccine effectiveness for those who are more than 40 years of old against serious COVID-19-related illness, and deaths for those who received 3rd dose of vaccine, at least 5 months after the 2nd dose.

The ideal gap between two doses of a vaccine

Data from the Oxford-AstraZeneca COVID-19 vaccine study, published in a peer-reviewed journal, concluded that a longer gap between two doses of vaccine work much better. The W.H.O also recommends an interval of four to twelve weeks for this vaccine. India extended the dose interval to six to eight weeks in March 2021.

A recent study shows that two doses of the AstraZeneca vaccine, administered 44-45 weeks apart, produced about four times the levels of antibodies, than when the doses were given 8-12 weeks apart. The antibody levels remain elevated for about one year, and interestingly, a third booster dose of vaccine (ChAdOx1 nCoV-19) given to a subset of volunteers, further boosted antibody levels to 2-fold compared to second dose. A subset of volunteers who received their second dose 15-25 weeks after the first dose, exhibited average antibody levels, at about 2-fold higher compared to those in the 8-12 week interval. This further suggests that lengthening the duration between vaccine doses tends to boost antibody levels.

The National Technical Advisory Group on Immunization (NTAGI) in India recommends increasing the gap between two shots of Covishield (Serum Institute of India and National Institute of Virology, ICMR) from twelve to sixteen weeks. Since Covishield is a replication-competent viral-vectored vaccine, when it is administered to an individual, the adenovirus enters the host cells, multiples and make copies of the antigenic portion (spike protein) in the body, to generate an immune response, which may be enough to provide adequate protection with a single dose, though at a lower level, and for a limited duration. This is very different from the inactivated or killed vaccines, such as Covaxin, made by the Bharat Biotech Private Limited, India, where there is no chance of making more copies of the spike proteins in the host cells. Therefore, in case of Covaxin, the first dose merely primes the immune system, and the second shot should be administered in a timely manner of four to six weeks, to boost the immune system.

Moreover, CDC, USA has quoted a recent study of almost 4,000 healthcare workers, that a single dose of the two vaccines (Pfizer-BioNTech and Moderna-NIH) is 80 per cent effective, in preventing infections, and two doses in an interval of 28 days are better with protection, jumping to 90 per cent two weeks, after the second shot. According to a recent press release, by the manufacturer of the vaccine Sputnik-V, Gamaleya Research Center, Russia, the interval between first and the second dose of vaccine even prolong the effect of the vaccine, without interfering with the immune response, spurred by the vaccine. It is possible to increase the minimum interval between the first and second doses from the previously approved 21 days to three months.

Does mix and match of two different vaccines produce higher immune response?

According to a new research by Oxford research group, mixing doses of AstraZeneca and Pfizer-Biotech vaccines elicits a strong immune response against COVID-19. The research compared the efficacy of having two vaccine shots of one kind, and mixed vaccines. The study revealed combination dose of AstraZeneca and Pfizer-BioNtech produced higher antibody levels compared to giving just two AstraZeneca vaccine shots. The study also found that two doses of Pfizer-BioNTech generated the best immune responses. The findings could allow flexibility of global vaccine rollout, letting people to receive whatever vaccine shot is available.

However, the concern is, what will happen if people need a third dose to prolong immunity or protection against emerging COVID-19 variants. Repeated doses of virus-based vaccines, such as Oxford-AstraZeneca, might result immune response, against the vaccine vector adenovirus, and thereby reducing the efficacy of the vaccine. A UK study, called Com-COV, which analyzed combinations of the two same vaccines, found that people in the mix-and-match groups experienced higher levels of vaccine-related adverse effects, such as fever compared to people, who received two doses of the same vaccine.

Furthermore, facing an acute crisis of shortage of doses for mass vaccination against COVID-19 in India, NTAGI has begun to explore the efficacy of a vaccine regimen that mixes two different types of COVID vaccines, such as Covishield and Covaxin, to determine if combination of two vaccines elicits stronger immune responses in individuals.

Does vaccine work in immunocompromised individuals?

Millions of people around the world are at a higher risk of becoming seriously ill from COVID-19 because they are immunocompromised.

The question is whether vaccines are effective in producing effective immune responses in those who have impaired immune system. And, also, whether it is safe to administer vaccine shots in immunocompromised individuals.

It is known that people who are highly immunocompromised can not have certain vaccines, such as vaccine against measles, mumps and rubella, as vaccine contains weakened live viruses that are too deleterious for people with damaged immune systems (CDC, USA). It is possible that the Pfizer-BioNTech and Moderna-NIH vaccines that contain only the genetic instruction for a single protein specific to SARS-CoV-2 virus, and not as a component of a whole vector virus, they might be safe for this group to receive either vaccine.

However, it is not about toxicity, but rather is the person going to elicit an immune response or not? People can be immunocompromised as they have certain autoimmune diseases, such as rheumatoid arthritis, lupus, T1D that impairs the self- and non-self recognition ability of the body's immune system, and let diseased individuals attack healthy adult tissue as opposed to protecting from infections. Furthermore, immunosuppression can be caused by medications, such as corticosteroids, and disease-modifying antirheumatic drugs (DMARDs), including some new biologics, that reduce inflammation, control pain, and further impair the internal immune system of the body. Having said that, even though immunocompromised patients have impaired immune system that respond less robustly to vaccination, it is possible that vaccines can provide some degree of protection against COVID-19 which is way better than no protection at all.

Furthermore, how well the vaccines work will depend upon each patient's overall state of immunosuppression at the time of receiving two doses of vaccine. Even if some of them get vaccinated, may still need to take extra precautions after vaccination (CDC, USA). Also, if someone has a condition or taking medications that weaker his/her immune system, the person may not be fully protected, even after fully vaccinated. For instance, one study found that among 7,000 patients who had Crohn's disease and ulcertative colitis, less than 50 per cent of those who were taking Remicade as treatment mounted an immune response following COVID-19 infection. Further, in follow up to that study, the researcher observed that about 34 per cent of people on the drug were protected after one dose of Pfizer-BioNTech vaccine, and just 27 per cent were protected after a single dose of the AstraZeneca vaccine. Moreover, CDC, USA studies that compared antibody response after 1st and 2nd dose of mRNA vaccine demonstrated less robust antibody response after 1st vaccine dose in individuals with various types of immunocompromising conditions.

Passive immunization

In contrast to active immunity that refers to the process of exposing the individual to an antigen (either natural or vaccine-mediated) to generate an adaptive immune response, passive immunity/immunization refers to the transfer of antibodies from one immunized individual to another non-immune individual. Interestingly, passive immunity occurs naturally, when maternal antibodies are transferred to the fetus, through the placenta or from breast milk to the gut of the infant. Moreover, it can be produced in the lab settings, when readymade antibody preparations derived from the sera of the immunized donors, or more recently, monoclonal antibodies (mAbs) or other antibodies, using several antibody-producing platforms, are transferred through systemic or mucosal route to non-immune individuals. Passive immunization is an attractive approach to confer immunity to those individuals who have impaired immune system or immunocompromised, and unable to make antibodies, using its own immune system. However, the transferred antibodies stay active for a limited time period in the recipients, and are unable to mount an effective memory B- and T-cell responses in the patients, as compared to active vaccination.

Convalescent plasma therapy (CPT)

In this approach, antibodies from the blood of the people, who had recovered from an infectious disease, such as COVID-19, transferred to another individual, through passive immunization, who recently contracted COVID-19 infection, and has symptoms. Historically, filtered plasma from the blood of recovered flu patients has been used in the past. It was used in the Spanish Flu pandemic of 1918-1919, and had shown to save lives. ICMR has initially approved CPT as an investigational therapy when vaccines against COVID-19 were not available. Thus, a few clinical trial sites for CPT and plasma bank have been set up in India. The early analyses on few clinical trials in India did not show much benefit. More studies are needed to determine the effectiveness of plasma therapy for the treatment of COVID-19 patients.

Monoclonal antibody therapy

Since the beginning of the worldwide COVID-19 disease, due to non-availability of vaccines for the general population in most countries, laboratory-made mAb, emerges a viable therapeutic option, to treat COVID-19 patients, and its complications, especially in older individuals, who have less efficient immune system due to inflammaging (senescence of immune cells with age) and/or immunocompromised. Till date, more than 50 mAb-related clinical trials are being conducted around the world to treat COVID-19 disease with few of them are close to completing the third and fourth phase of clinical trial. Most of the mAb's are directed against spike protein of the SARS-CoV-2. The mAbs gained media attention in October 2020, when Donald Trump received the experimental Regeneron (USA) antibody cocktail treatment. They have since progressed to allow more widespread use. Regeneron developed a "combination antibody cocktail" called REGN-COV2,which contains the mAbs casirivimab and imdevimab. These data support the use of REGN-COV to prevent COVID-19 in uninfected individuals including immunocompromised people who typically do not respond adequately to vaccines. The phase III clinical trials showed that a single dose of REGN-COV antibody treatment reduced the risk of contracting COVID-19 by 81.6 per cent two to eight months after administration. Moreover, the antibody treatment reduced the risk by 81.4 per cent one month after administration. Also, Eli Lilly and Company (Indianapolis, USA), developed two different antibody therapies: bamlanivimab monotherapy, and combination bamlanivimab and etesevimab therapy. The FDA (The Food and Drug Administration, USA) has authorized the emergency use of combined bamlanivimab and etesevimab for people with mild-to-moderate COVID-19. Also, the Russian biotechnology company BIOCAD developed the antibody levilimab (Ilsira) that targets pro-inflammatory cytokine IL-6 (interleukin-6) to prevent cytokine storm-related complications, caused by COVID-19. Tocilizumab, another mAb that has received approval from the FDA to treat rheumatologic disorders, yet to have authorization from the FDA to treat COVID-19. The NIH (National Institute of Health, USA), however, recommends these antibodies for hospitalized COVID-19 patients on the condition that healthcare professionals use them in conjunction with other conventional medication, such as dexamethasone.

Cross-reactive immunity from vaccines

Our ability to fight against a novel deadly pathogen, such as virus, depends in part, on the effectiveness of cross-reactive pre-existing T cell immunity. If we have enough cross- reactive T cells, due to prior vaccination against some other diseases, we do not necessarily need to catch a novel virus, such as COVID-19 as the T cells know how to fight it, as prior exposure to similar viruses or vaccine against it had taught immune system how to respond to this new one. T-cell receptors (TCR) recognize peptides presented by the MHC (Major Histocompatibility Complex) on the surface of APCs. The ability of TCR to recognize more than one peptide-MHC structure confers cross-reactivity. The discrepancy between the high numbers of pathogen-derived peptides and the lower diversity of the T-cell repertoire, and the presence of many intrinsic low affinity receptors, explain, in part, the cross-reactivity.

Vaccines available for other diseases prevent COVID-19?

There is some epidemiological evidence that shows that prior vaccination with BCG or measles may have some protection against developing COVID-19 disease, due to the presence of cross-reactive T cells, that recognize key COVID-19 immunogenic components. However, this is primarily based on what is called ecological evidence, where results are estimated based on population, and not individuals, that means the evidence is weak and inconclusive. There are ongoing studies on vaccines, such as BCG, recombinant BCG, polio, and measles to determine if they have any protective effect or disease modifying in COVID-19 patients that will provide more evidence to come up with a clear answer.

Figure 3. Structure and Function of Antibody: Antibody is consisting of four polypeptide chains: two identical heavy chains (H) and two identical light (L) chains. The light and the heavy chains are linked by disulfide bonds to reconstitute the arms of a Y-shaped structure and each arm is known as Fab. The Fab is composed of two variable domains; VH and VL and two constant domains; CH1 and CL. When the light and heavy chains are paired, the two variable domains dimerize to form the Fv fragment that recognizes the Ag binding site. Each variable domain consists of 6 hypervariable loops, three in the heavy chain (H1, H2, and H3) and three in the light chain (L1, L2, and L3) intermingled by a conserved FR of β-sheets. Two additional domains of the heavy chain, CH2, and CH3, compose the Fc region that mediates some of the biological activities of the Ab molecule in a non-specific manner. (A) The 3-D structure of an Ab molecule. (B) A schematic representation of the Ab scaffold.

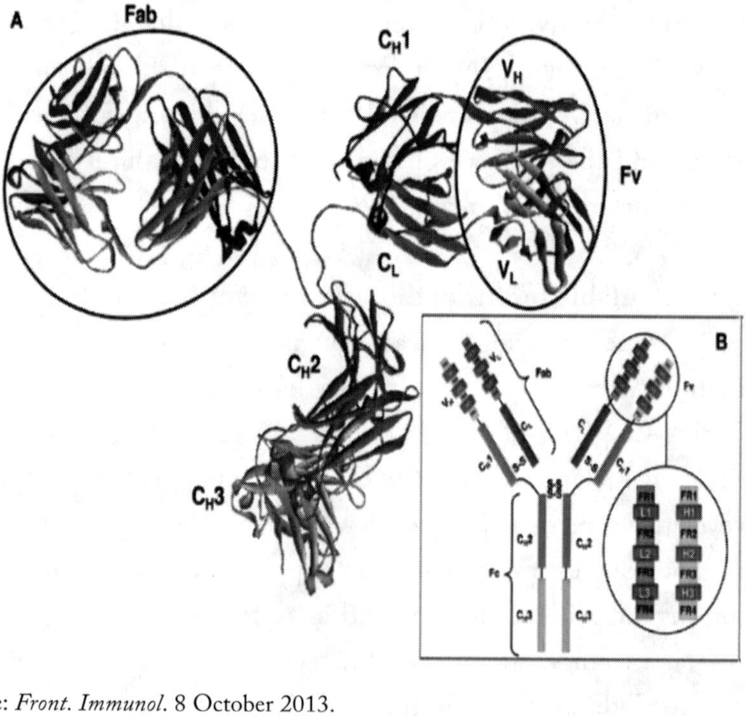

Source: *Front. Immunol.* 8 October 2013.

Figure 4. The underlying molecular mechanisms of cell-mediated innate immune activation upon SARS-CoV-2 infection: SARS-CoV-2 enters host cells through interactions between the surface unit of spike protein (S) and host Angiotensin-Converting Enzyme 2 (ACE2) and Transmembrane protease, serine 2 (TMPRSS2), followed by endocytosis and viral genome release; positive-sense single-stranded RNA (ss+RNA) into the cytosol. As virus replicates, the intermediate double-stranded RNA are recognized as Pathogen-associated molecular pattern molecules (PAMPs) by various host pattern recognition receptors (PRRs), such as MDA5 (melanoma differentiation-associated protein), LGP2 (laboratory of genetics and physiology), and NOD1 (nucleotide-binding oligomerisation domain containing 1). Subsequently, PRRs activate a multitude of downstream components through signal transduction mediated by MAVS (Mitochondrial antiviral-signaling protein), resulting activation of kinases, such as IKKε (Inhibitor of κ-B kinase ε and TBK1 (TANK-binding kinase 1). These kinases phosphorylates IRF3 (Interferon regulatory factor 3), which dimerises and translocates to the nucleus where it actives transcription factors (NF-κB, IRF3, IRF5) to activate transcription of genes encoding type 1 interferon. It bonds to host cell type 1 receptors with extracellular domains that bind type 1 interferon, leading to a molecular cascade through the JAK-STAT (Jenus kinase-signal transducer and activator of transcription) pathway leading to effective binding of the STAT1-STAT2-IRF9 heterodimer to the ISRE (interferon-stimulated response sequence) and subsequent stimulation of ISGs (interferon-stimulated genes), that elicit various antiviral effects.

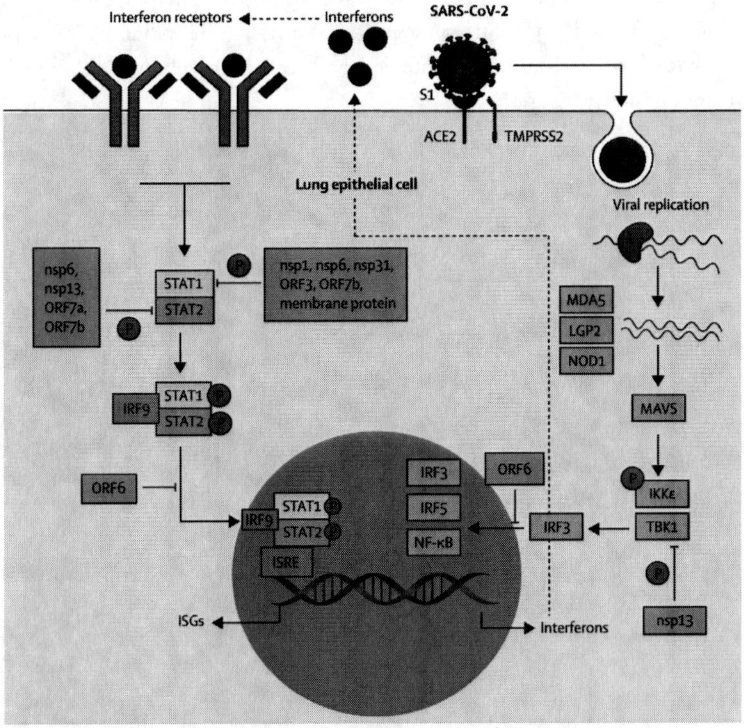

Source: The Lancet Respiratory Medicine, October 21, 2021.

Figure 5. An overview of adaptive immune response to SARS-CoV-2: SARS-CoV-2-infected epithelial cells leads to the production of proinflammatory cytokines, Antigen presenting cells, such as dendritic cells (DCs) recognize PAMPs and inflammatory markers (eg, interferons), leading to their activation. Activated DCs migrate to the lymph nodes and present antigen (on MHC class I or class II molecules) and co-stimulatory molecules to immature T-cells, which subsequently differentiates into CD8+ cytotoxic T lymphocytes, CD4+ T cells, or Tfh (T follicular helper) cells; all of which can differentiate into long-term memory cells. Tfh cells interact with and activate B lymphocytes, which differentiate into plasma cells or memory B cells that produce high-affinity antibodies to specific viral antigen such as spike protein of SARS-CoV-2. Viral antigens processed in phagolysosomes of infected epithelial cells are presented on the cell surface via MHC molecules. Peripheral cytotoxic T lymphocytes recognize antigen-containing MHC class I molecule via their CD8 co-receptors, and interactions between CD8-T-Cell co-receptors and MHC class I molecules activate cytotoxic T lymphocytes, leading to the release of proinflammatory cytokines together with cytotoxic granules, such as granzymes, that trigger apoptosis of the infected host cells. However, SARS-CoV-2 can hinder adaptive immune response through the accessory protein ORF8 (open reading frame) localizes in lysosomes by down regulating the trafficking of MHC class I molecules to the surface of epithelial cells causing reduction of cytotoxic-T-lymphocytes-mediated killing of infected host cells and subsequent activation of downstream immune activation.

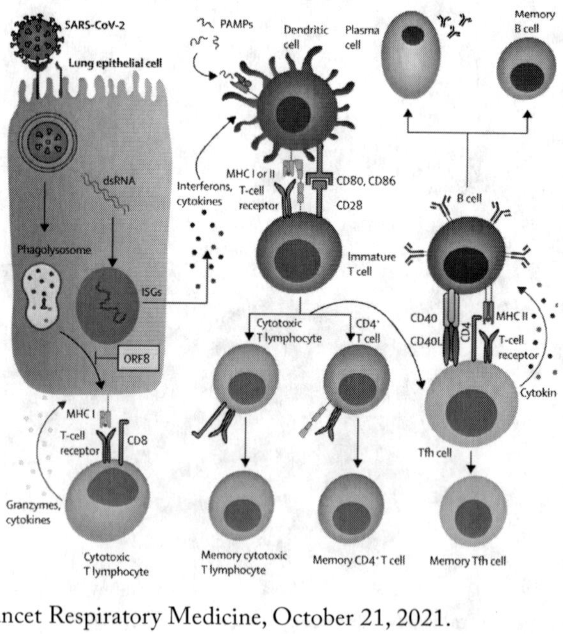

Source: The Lancet Respiratory Medicine, October 21, 2021.

Figure 6. Cumulative incidence curves comparing COVID-19-related admission to hospital **(A),** severe disease **(B),** and death **(C)** in individuals who received two versus three doses of the BNT162b2 COVID-19 vaccine. The dashed vertical lines indicate the day 7, on which the main analysis period begins.

(A)

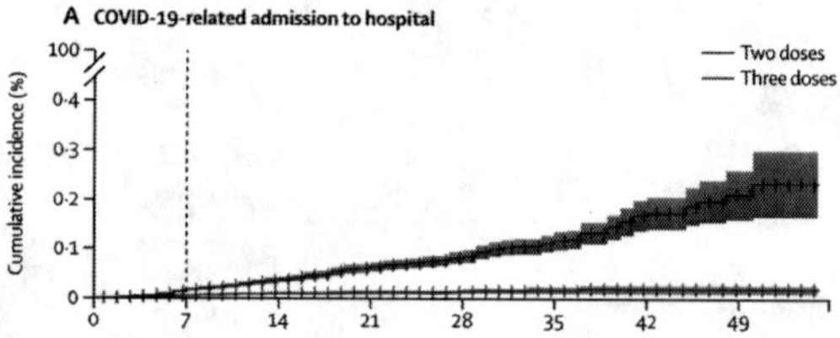

Number at risk									
Two doses	728 321	471 082	301 296	202 547	107 638	47 619	21 759	6368	..
Three doses	728 321	471 181	301 542	202 900	108 036	48 018	22 071	6502	..
Cumulative number of events									
Two doses	0	91	167	229	259	282	299	303	..
Three doses	0	31	46	51	54	56	57	57	..

(B)

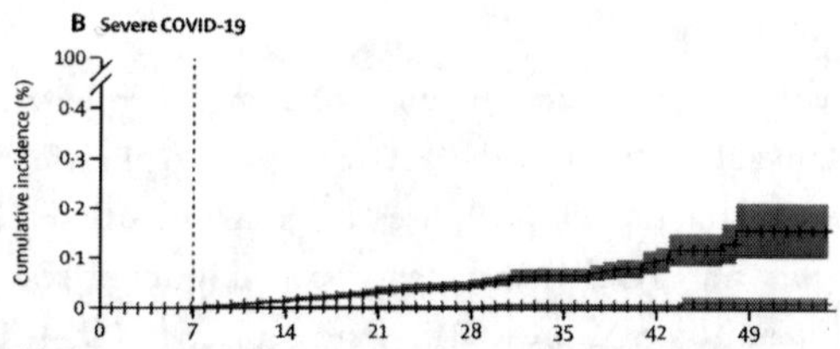

Number at risk								
Two doses	728 321	471 147	301 395	202 655	107 748	47 709	21 839	6400
Three doses	728 321	471 200	301 561	202 919	108 050	48 025	22 076	6504
Cumulative number of events								
Two doses	0	12	71	116	135	149	158	165
Three doses	0	10	14	18	20	22	22	23

(C)

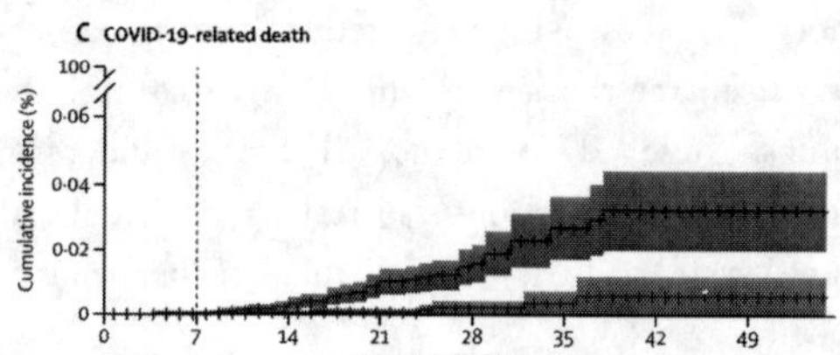

Number at risk								
Two doses	728 321	471 153	301 443	202 735	107 836	47 796	21 911	6435
Three doses	728 321	471 205	301 567	202 924	108 056	48 030	22 078	6505
Cumulative number of events								
Two doses	0	2	13	29	36	44	46	46
Three doses	0	0	2	3	5	6	7	7

Source: *The Lancet*, October 29, 2021.

Figure 7. Per cent of subjects with antibody response after two mRNA COVID-19 vaccine doses by immunocompromising condition and study (n=63). Antibody measurements and threshold level vary by study protocol.

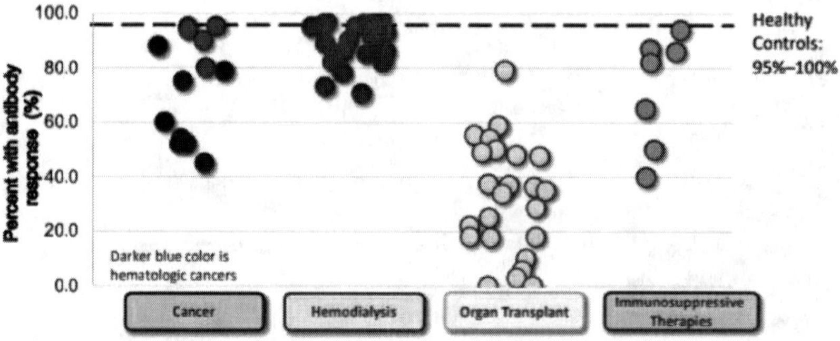

- Studies that compared response after 1st and 2nd dose demonstrated less robust response after dose 1
- **Antibody measurement and threshold levels vary by study protocol**

Source: Center for Disease Control and Prevention, USA.

Figure 8. Schematic models of the three major scenarios wherein cross-reactive CD4+ memory T cells are able to control the SARS-CoV-2 replication in an individual, and reduce the severity of the COVID-19 disease: Timelines of viral load in the lungs and the upper respiratory tract (UTR) and the associated immune responses against it based on the magnitude and type of pre-existing cross-reactive CD4+ T cell memory. Each of these models is currently hypothetical for SARS-CoV-2. Model 1 hypothesizes that reduction of lung viral load and disease symptoms through cross-reactive CD4+ memory T cell from previous SARS-related infection (not SARS-CoV-2), but have minimal impact on UTR vital load. Model 2 assumes that memory T_{FH} cells facilitate a faster, robust neutralizing antibody response against SARS-CoV-2 than would occur in the absence of memory T_{FH} cells. Model 3 predicts the probability of the cross-reactive CD4+ T_{RM} cells present at the site of infection to control the viral load rapidly in the UTR and lungs. These CD4+ memory T cells would restrict viral replication in the UTR after infection and possibly also restrict viral replication through activation of innate immune system. T_{FH} = T follicular helper cells, T_{RM}= Tissue-resident memory cells.

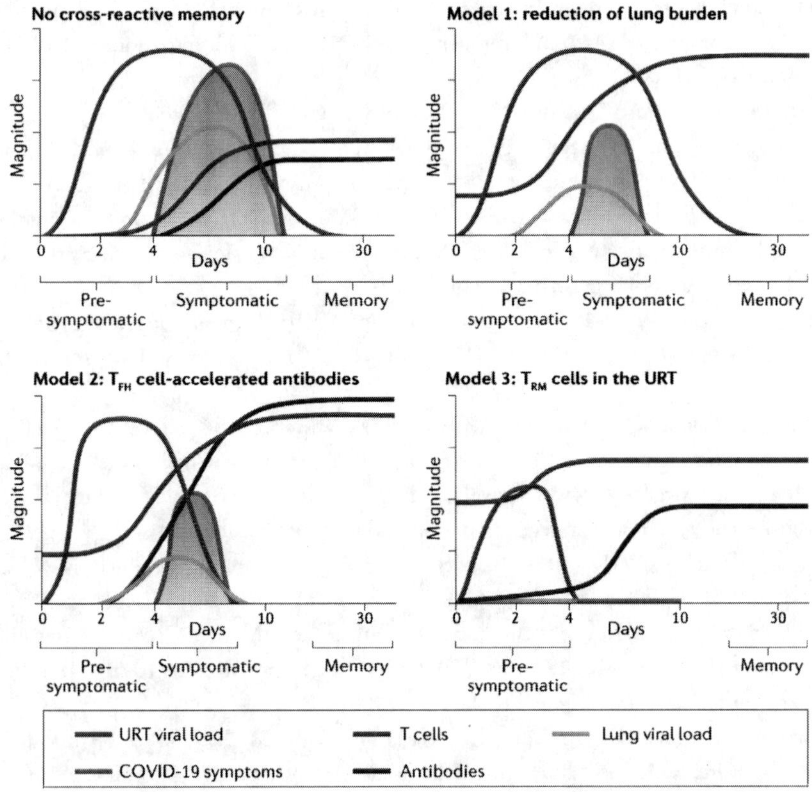

Source: *Nature Reviews Immunology,* 20, 709-713 (2020).

References

Innate immunity. R. Medzhitov, and C. Janeway, Jr. *N Engl J Med* 2000; 343:338-344. DOI: https://doi.org/10.1056/NEJM200008033430506

Does infection with or vaccination against SARS-COV-2 lead to lasting immunity? G. Milne et al. *THE LANCET Respiratory Medicine*, Oct 21, 2021. DOI: https://doi.org/10.1016/S2213-2600(21)00407-0.

COVID-19 Genomics UK (COG-UK) Consortiium1. Exponential growth, high prevalence of SARS-CoV-2, and vaccine effectiveness associated with the Delta variant. P. Elliot et al. *Science* 2021; eabl9551. DOI: https://doi.org/10.1126/science.abl9551.

Efficacy of the mRNA-1273 SARS-CoV-2 vaccine at completion of blinded phase. EL Sahly et al. *N Engl J Med,* September 22, 2021. DOI: https://doi.org/10.1056/NEJMoa2113017.

Understanding Breakthrough Infections Following mRNA SARS-CoV-2 Vaccination. M Klompas. *JAMA*, November 4, 2021. DOI: https://doi.org/10.1001/jama.2021.19063.

Effectiveness of a third dose of BNT162b2 mRNA COVID-19 vaccine for preventing severe outcomes in Israel: an observational study. N. Barda et al. *The Lancet*, October 29, 2021. DOI: https://doi.org/10.1016/S0140-6736(21)02249-2.

Viral loads of Delta-variant SARS-CoV-2 breakthrough infections after vaccination and boosters with BNT162b2. M. Levine-Tiefenbrun et al. *Nature Medicine* (2021). DOI: https://doi.org/10.1038/s41591-021-01575-4.

Expert Discuss COVID-19 Variants and Vaccine Efficacy, Immunosuppressed Patients, and More. *JAMA*. 2021; 325(17): 1711-1712. DOI: https://doi.org/10.1001/jama.2021.5938.

Antibody Cocktail Could Reduce COVID Risk by Nearly 82 per cent, Regeneron Trial Shows. Newsweek. 08 November 2021. https://www.newsweek-com.cdn.ampproject.org/c/s/www.newsweek.com/antibody-cocktail-could-reduce-covid-risk-nearly-82-per cent-regeneron-trial-shows-1646995?amp=1

Mix- and Match COVID vaccines trigger potent immune response. E. Callaway. *Nature* 593, 491 (2021). DOI: https://doi.org/10.1038/d41586-021-01359-3

The Evolution of Adaptive Immunity. Z. Pancer and M. D. Cooper. *Annu Rev Immunol.* Vol. 24: 497-518, 2006. DOI: https://doi.org/10.1146/annurev.immunol.24.021605.0

Humoral Immunity Due to Long-Lived Plasma Cells. M.K. Slifka, R. Antia, J. K. Whitmire, R. Ahmed. *Immunity*. Vol.8. Issue 3, Pages 363-372,1998. DOI: https://doi.org/10.1016/S1074-7613(00)80541-5

Secondary mechanisms of diversification in the human antibody repertoire. B.S. Briney, J.E. Crowe Jr. *Front Immunol.*, 11 March 2013. DOI: https://doi.org/10.3389/fimmu.2013.00042

Immunological memory to SARS-CoV-2 assessed for up to 8 months after infection. J.M. Dan, J. Mateus et al. *Science* 5 Feb 2021. Vol. 371, Issue 6529. DOI: https://doi.org/10.1126/science.abf4063

Neutralizing Antibodies Against SARS-CoV-2 Variants After Infection and Vaccination. V.V. Edara, W. H. Hudson, X. Xie et al. *JAMA*. 2021; 325(18):1896-1898. DOI: https://doi.org/10.1001/jama.2021.4388

T Cell Vaccination. I.R. Cohen, in Encyclopedia of immunology (Second Edition), 1998.

Passive Immunization. M.K. Slifka and I.J. Amanna. Plotkin's Vaccines. 2018: 84-95.e10. DOI: https://doi.org/10.1016/B978-0-323-35761-6.00008-0

Vaccination of immunocompromised patients. P. Ljungman. *Clin Microbiol Infect*. 2012 Oct; 18 Suppl 5:93-9. DOI: https://doi.org/10.1111/j.1469-0691.2012.03971.x.

Monoclonal Antibodies for COVID-19. E. C. Lloyd, T.N. Gandhi, L.A. Petty. *JAMA*. 2021; 325(10): 1015. DOI: https://doi.org/10.1001/jama.2021.1225

Convalescent plasma transfusion for the treatment of COVID-19: Systematic review. K. Rajendran et al. *J Med Virol.* 2020 Sep; 92(9): 1475-1483. DOI: https://doi.org/10.1002/jmv.25961

Cross-Reactivity of T Cells and Its Role in the Immune System. G. Petrova, A. Ferrante, J. Gorski. *Crit Rev Immunol.* 2012; 32(4): 349-372.

Cross-reactive memory T cells and herd immunity to SARS-CoV-2. M. Lipsitch et al. *Nat Rev Immunol* 20, 709-713 (2020). DOI: https://doi.org/10.1038/s41577-020-00460-4.

Vaccine Efficacy

> "If a vaccine that was developed that is 50 per cent effective in preventing Covid, it would still be licensed."
>
> – The New York Times

> "What this [COVID] virus continued to demonstrate is its ability to find people who are not vaccinated."
>
> – Star Tribune, September 28, 2021

> "These [COVID] vaccines are safer than aspirin…vaccines still remain number one, two, three, four, and five tool to stop the pandemic."
>
> – St. Peter Herald, September 2, 2021

Simplistically, vaccine efficacy is defined by its effectiveness in reducing the percentage risk of developing a disease in the vaccinated individuals, enrolled in a clinical trial, as compared to unvaccinated ones. It differs from vaccine effectiveness in real world that measures how well a vaccine works, when given to people in a community.

The various phases of clinical trials

Clinical trials involve testing an experimental drug, vaccine etc. to assess the safety, and efficacy of the intervention. Clinical trials are carefully designed, incorporating many inclusion and exclusion criteria for study participants, and extensively reviewed by the IEC for its approval. If the clinical trial is for a new product, most countries require that all phases of testing approved by the regulatory authority, before they can begin, but in some countries, early stages of testing can be done without regulatory approval.

Vaccine research can be grouped into two phases: preclinical and clinical.

Preclinical stage: This is a stage prior to human testing. The purpose of these studies is to demonstrate that the vaccines are safe in animals. If animal models of a disease are available, the efficacy of the vaccines in preventing infection, and disease may also be tried. Preclinical toxicity studies are typically done in mice or rabbits, whereas immunogenicity studies are done in other species, such as guinea pigs, and hamsters.

Clinical stage: Human clinical trials are done in three phases:

Phase I: This is done on a small number (about 20-40) of healthy adult individuals to assess the safety of the vaccine. Participants are followed up for weeks.

Phase II: The clinical investigators give vaccine to a few hundred participants to assess the safety in a large number, and measure immunogenicity. This phase is also used to decide what dose should be ideal. Typically, the participants are equally divided using randomization into two halves; one group gets actual vaccine and the other group gets mock vaccine or placebo. This stage of the trial lasts a few weeks to several months, depending on how many doses of the vaccine need to be given, since the final immune response can only be determined in two to four weeks after the last dose of the vaccine is given.

Phase III: This phase is needed to determine the efficacy of the vaccine. The vaccine is administered into tens of thousands of people, with some given the vaccine, and the others the placebo. The aim is to make sure that there is no bias in who gets the vaccine and who does not in either single- or double-blinded placebo- controlled, randomized clinical trial (RCT). The research team compares the two groups to see if vaccinated people witness less severity of the disease than the unvaccinated people. In general, phase III trial may take years.

Finally, after successful completion of all the phases of clinical trials, if the vaccine is found to be safe and effective, the clinical data are submitted to the national regulatory authority along with very detailed information how it is made, and tested at every stage of the production. The regulatory authority examines the data, and decides on the licensing. Even when the vaccine is licensed for public use and widely administered, the vaccine makers are required to collect and submit the safety data from the general public, known as post-marketing surveillance, that is sometimes referred to as Phase IV of vaccine trials.

"Human challenge trials" or controlled human infection model

The most common bottlenecks in vaccine development are cost, risk, safety, and time. It is possible that a new vaccine shows early promise in a preclinical or Phase I trial. However, if any one of those factors (cost, risk, safety, and time) is not aligning with the goal of the researchers involved in the trial, it is often difficult to move forward with the vaccine candidate. Interestingly, clinical models, such as human challenge trial provide an excellent opportunity to move past these bottlenecks. Typically, in Phase III conventional clinical trials, the efficacy of a vaccine can be reliably assessed only when the vaccinated and unvaccinated individuals are exposed to the pathogen unknowingly, and breakthrough (re-infection) infections are measured. However, the natural infection is unpredictable and dependent on the environments. Thus, it takes enormous time for natural infection to happen that delays the measurement of the vaccine efficacy.

In the human challenge trials, healthy volunteers are intentionally challenged, or infected with an infectious agent. This lets researchers to study the effect of a vaccination on the disease itself in a controlled environment. The participants stay on-site for the entire duration of the trial, and fully staffed analytical laboratory and medical professionals can provide priority access to any care participants may need. In this model, almost all experimental parameters, such as the challenge agents, inclusion and exclusion criteria, the schedule of assessments, the dose of the infectious agents administered, and the timing of the inoculation are controlled. Therefore, in human challenge trials are effective on a small participant pool that faces minimal risk of adverse outcomes, clinical complications or hospitalization. Importantly, the small size of the trial reduces the financial risk of failure, cost, as much less vaccine is required for a human challenge trial than a Phase II clinical trial. The W.H.O has developed ethical guidelines on the use of controlled human infection models in SARS-CoV-2 in consultation with multiple stakeholders, where half of them have agreed on the usefulness of this model, and the others have reservations about its usefulness.

Determination of vaccine efficacy

Vaccine efficacy is typically determined in a controlled clinical setting. For example, the Pfizer-BioNTech study for determining the efficacy of its COVID-19 vaccine had enrolled 43,661 volunteers. Half of them were given a placebo and the other half was given the vaccine. The study used randomization to divide equally the 43,661 subjects into placebo group and the vaccine group. In the placebo group, 162 became infected with COVID-19 and showed symptoms. In the vaccine group, the number was just 8 (breakthrough infection). The per cent infection risk of the placebo group was 162 divided by 21,830 and multiplied by 100= 0.74% and for vaccinated group was 8 divided by 21,830 and multiplied by 100= 0.04%. The number of people expected to contract the virus is unvaccinated will be 2, 427,200 (0.0074 multiplied by the total population number of the U.S. (328 million). The number of people expected to contract the virus if vaccinated will be 131,200 only (0.0004 multiplied by the total population number of the U.S. (328 million). Thus, the vaccine reduced the risk by 0.7% (0.74%- 0.04%) that seems small. However, when scaled up this difference with the infection risk of placebo group (0.7% divided by 0.74%), the number became 0.9459 (about 95%). It means the vaccine reduces the risk of infection by 95 per cent that is vaccine efficacy.

As per regulatory agencies, a vaccine should have at least 50 per cent efficacy in the clinical trial to be allowed for mass vaccination. That means the results of the trial should show prevention of at least half of the disease. Having said that, because of the size of the trials, it is possible that the actual efficacy of the vaccine may be higher or lower. Thus, a study to measure the real-world effectiveness of a vaccine, previously determined by the clinical trial, should be assessed from the results of mass vaccination. Nonetheless, an imperfect vaccine will still protect a large proportion of people. Also, once a few vaccines are available, researchers can focus on improving their performance.

Figure 9. Estimated effectiveness of vaccines in preventing COVID-19 based on interim data from late-stage clinical trials.

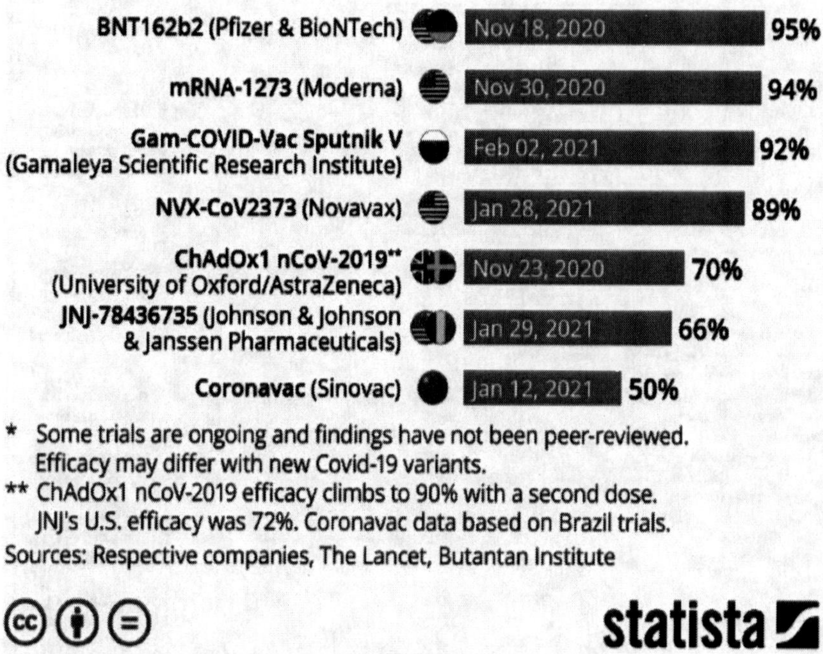

Source: Statista.

Figure 10. Efficacy of mRNA-1273 vaccine (Moderna-NIH) in preventing COVID-19 in subgroups.

Subgroup	Placebo (N=14,164)	mRNA-1273 (N=14,287)	Vaccine Efficacy (95% CI)
	no. of events/total no.		*percent*
Overall	744/14,164	55/14,287	93.2 (91.0 to 94.8)
Age			
≥18 to <65 yr	644/10,569	46/10,661	93.4 (91.1 to 95.1)
≥65 yr	100/3595	9/3626	91.5 (83.2 to 95.7)
≥65 to <75 yr	81/2898	9/2990	89.7 (79.6 to 94.9)
≥75 yr	19/697	0/636	100.0 (NE to 100.0)
Sex			
Male	378/7494	30/7439	92.5 (89.1 to 94.8)
Female	366/6670	25/6848	93.8 (90.7 to 95.9)
Race or ethnic group			
White	631/11,273	48/11,391	93.0 (90.6 to 94.7)
Black	41/1352	4/1391	91.1 (75.2 to 96.8)
Asian	29/700	1/628	96.6 (74.2 to 99.5)
American Indian or Alaska Native	5/113	0/109	100.0 (NE to 100.0)
Native Hawaiian or other Pacific Islander	0/31	0/36	NE (NE to NE)
Hispanic or Latinx ethnicity			
Hispanic or Latinx	177/2787	10/2831	94.8 (90.2 to 97.3)
Not Hispanic or Latinx	563/11,249	45/11,322	92.6 (90.0 to 94.5)
Coexisting conditions			
Chronic lung disease	30/692	4/675	87.2 (63.8 to 95.5)
Significant cardiac disease	30/696	4/726	88.0 (65.9 to 95.8)
Severe obesity (BMI >40)	75/980	7/1009	91.4 (81.4 to 96.0)
Diabetes	72/1363	3/1402	96.2 (87.9 to 98.8)
Liver disease	5/90	1/100	81.0 (−64.8 to 97.8)
HIV	4/82	0/85	100.0 (NE to 100)
Occupational risk			
No risk	72/2480	4/2541	94.8 (85.8 to 98.1)
Health care providers	209/3261	13/361	94.4 (90.3 to 96.8)
Emergency response providers	25/273	2/287	93.0 (70.6 to 98.4)
Retail and restaurant workers	58/875	5/870	92.0 (80.0 to 96.8)
Manufacturing and production operators	21/390	2/390	90.9 (61.0 to 97.9)
Warehouse shipping and fulfillment center workers	13/158	2/174	86.1 (38.4 to 96.9)
Transportation and delivery service providers	22/428	2/428	91.3 (62.8 to 97.9)
Border protection and military personnel	3/66	0/64	100.0 (NE to 100)
Personal care and in-home service providers	29/413	2/417	93.5 (72.8 to 98.5)
Hospitality and tourism workers	10/200	3/214	74.1 (5.6 to 92.9)
Pastoral, social, or public health workers	36/485	1/506	97.6 (82.2 to 99.7)
Educator and students	77/1478	7/1476	91.3 (81.2 to 96.0)
Other	237/4506	23/4586	91.1 (86.3 to 94.2)

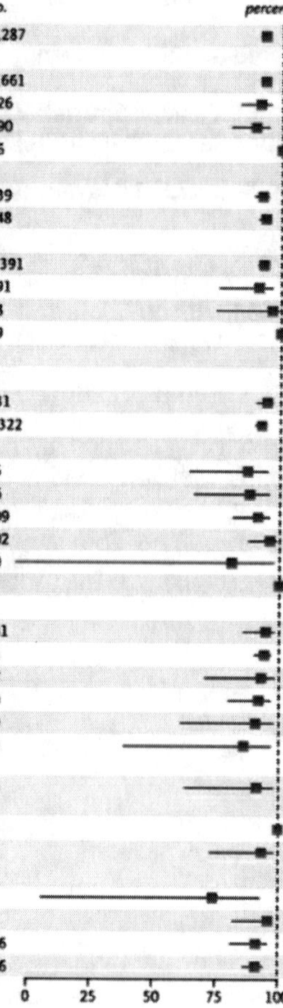

Source: *The New England Journal of Medicine,* 2021.

References

A New Vaccine to Battle Covid-19. B. F. Haynes. *N Engl J Med.* 2020 Dec 30: NEJMe2035557. DOI: https://doi.org/10.1056/NEJMe2025557.

What does 95% COVID-19 vaccine efficacy really mean? P. Olliaro. *THE LANCET Infectious Disease.* Vol. 21, Issue 6, P769, June 01, 2021. DOI: https://doi.org/10.1016/S1473-3099(21)00075-X.

Understanding COVID-19 vaccine efficacy. M. Lipsitch, N.E. Dean. *Science*, 2020-science.sciencemag.org.

Oxford-Astra Zeneca COVID-19 vaccine efficacy. M. D. Knoll, C. Wonodi. *The Lancet*. Vol. 397, Issue 10269, P72-74, January 09, 2021. DOI: https://doi.org/10.1016/S0140-6736(20)32623-4.

Efficacy and Safety of the mRNA-1273 SARS-CoV-2 Vaccine. L. R. Baden et al. *N Engl J Med* 2021; 384:403-416. DOI: https://doi.org/10.1056/NEJMoa2035389.

DESIGN AND ANALYSIS OF CLINICAL TRIALS. Concepts and Methodologies. Second Edition. S. C. Chow, J. P. Liu. A John Wiley & Sons, Inc, Publication.

PHASES OF CLINICAL TRIALS: A REVIEW. R. A. Singh, R. Kumar et al. *International Journal of Pharmaceutical, Chemical & Biological Sciences*. Jul-Sep2013, Vol. 3 Issue 3, P700-703. 4P.

The randomized controlled trial: gold standard, or merely standard? J. Grossman, F.J. Mackenzie-Perspectives in biology and medicine 48 (4), 516-534, 2005.

Human challenge trials in vaccine development. A. Sekhar, G. Kang. *Seminars in Immunology*, Vol. 50, August 2020, 101429. DOI: https://doi.org/10.1016/j.smim.2020.101429.

Exploring Risks of Human Challenge Trials For COVID-19. D. Manheim, W. Wiecek, V. Schmit, J. Morrison, 1Day Sooner Research Team. *Risk Analysis*. Vol. 41, Issue 5, P710-720, 2021. DOI: https://doi.org/10.1111/risa.13726.

Vaccine Nationalism

"Vaccine nationalism will prolong the pandemic, and not shorten it."
– Terods Adhanom Ghebreyesus

"Nationalism: An infantile disease. It is a measles of mankind."
–Albert Einstein

As COVID-19 vaccines are developed and approved, policy leaders around the world, face a critical dilemma: which to prioritize-country or planet? Vaccine nationalism is a critical goal of a country to make sure its majority of the citizens get vaccinated prior to exporting indigenous vaccines to other countries to vaccinate their population.

Thus, it ensures buying or making vaccines in advance, or through ordering its own vaccine manufacturers to reserve dose for its own citizens. However, it often adversely affects not only the global health recovery, but also the economy. Many developed countries have done bilateral deals with the vaccine manufacturing companies, to ensure that a certain number of doses are reserved for the country. Progress has been made through initiative, such as COVAX (COVID-19 Global Vaccine Access): the global effort to ensure access to COVID-19 vaccines for all countries. However, it is likely, the majority of the world's poor countries won't be able to get enough access to vaccine reserve.

The vaccine nationalism is not entirely new as a similar pattern was seen during the 2009 HIN1 influenza pandemic. Prior to that, vaccines for smallpox and polio were only available in developing nations, when developed countries had secured enough vaccine stocks for domestic needs.

Vaccine nationalism also leads to a prolonged pandemic, as only a handful of countries would get most of the supply, that may actually help the virus to spread more across the world. Also, vaccine nationalism is not ethically justified when there are four ventilators per million people in some low-income and middle-income countries. Thus, it is reasonable to argue, that rich countries can stockpile their vaccines to themselves to protect their population first.

Furthermore, national access to COVID-19 vaccines for the citizens has essentially become a priority in power politics, as a means to recover from the economic damage at home, in export markets, and in the context of strategic importance in the balance of power. It is not only the poorest countries will suffer, since, as long as the COVID-19 disease is not under control everywhere, the cost of the global pandemic will continue to be as high as USD 1.2 trillion per annum, according to a research done by a non-profit organization RAND Europe.

A tangible solution to this problem is to scale up the manufacturing of the vaccines. This requires vaccine IP (intellectual property) holding big pharmaceutical companies to release the patents. However, there is a need to pay the IP holder the technology-transfer fees and a fair price, as that is the capitalist incentive structure, under which it operates. This is stressful for any country, given the extra economic burden of lockdowns, weakened and overwhelmed healthcare system, it may be difficult to pay reasonable market price to vaccine manufacturers, and provide the mass population vaccines for free of cost.

Moreover, the current global vaccination rates of approximately 6.7 million doses per day translate to achieving herd immunity in about 4.6 years. Thus, it is likely, that the entire world would not be vaccinated for the next few years. It is wrong to assume that affluent countries can leave out of them from the worldwide pandemic by just vaccinating themselves. Due to increasing mobility of the population across many parts of the world, infection transmission from unvaccinated people in many countries, confer significant risk for people to become infected with the virus. In essence, ideally, the entire world needs to be vaccinated, and most effective vaccines against COVID-19 should be distributed across the world, irrespective of the economic disparities among countries.

Figure 11. Immunization promised to countries by income level.

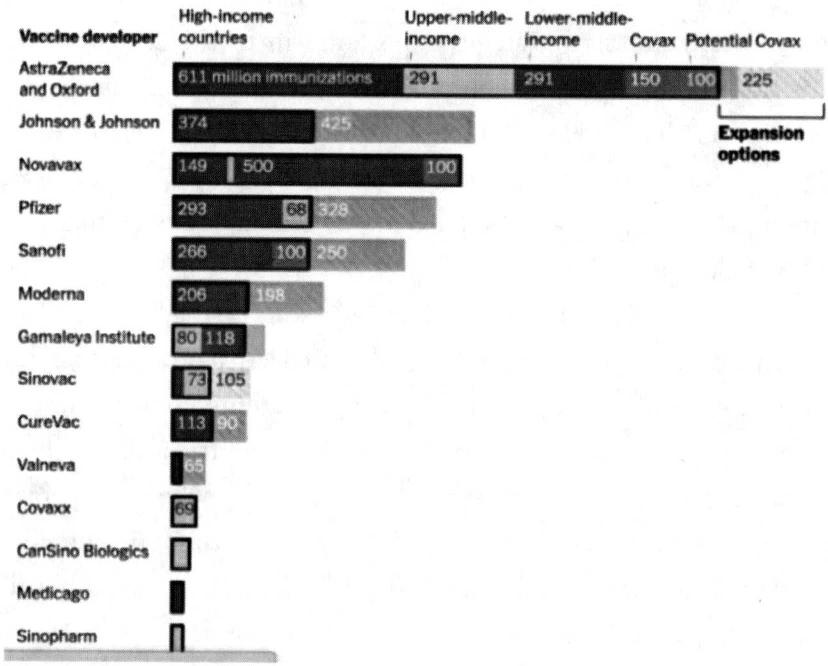

Source: The New York Times.

Figure 12. Vaccine preorders as a percentage of population.

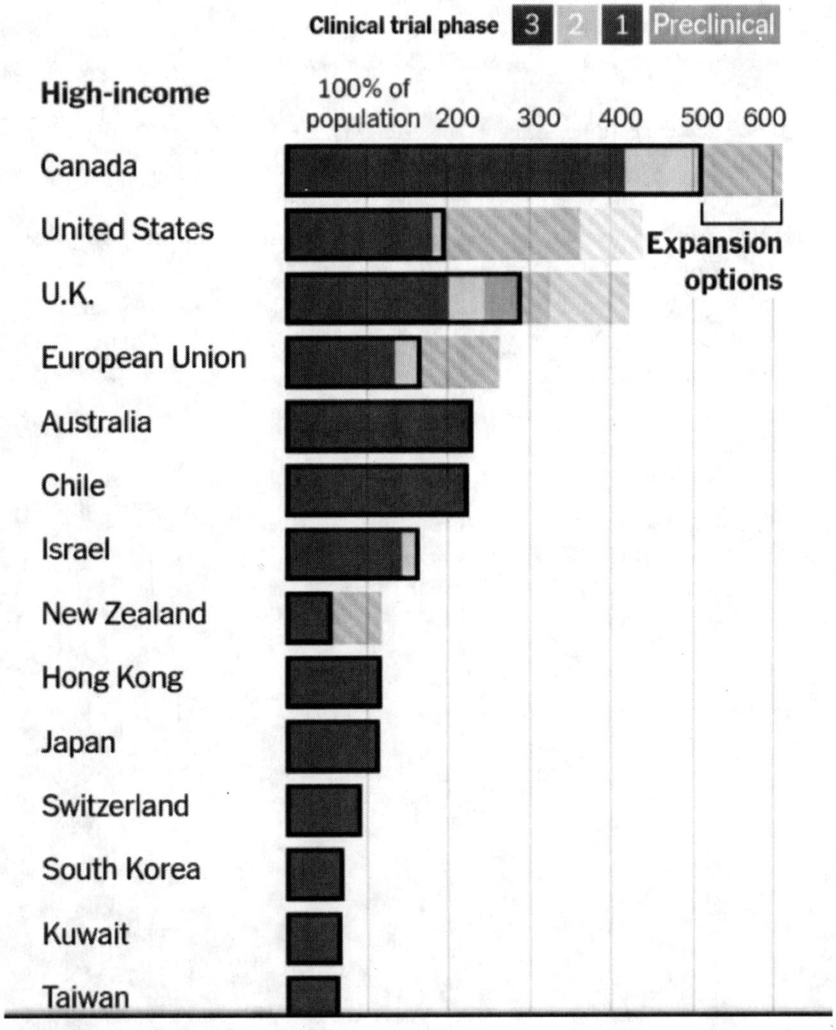

Source: The New York Times.

References

From Vaccine Nationalism to Vaccine Equity-Finding a Path Forward. I.T. Katz et al. *N Engl J Med* 2021; 384:1281-1282. DOI: https://doi.org/10.1056/NEJMp2103614

Against vaccine nationalism. N. Hassoun. *Journal of Medical Ethics*. DOI: http://dx.doi.org/10.1136/medethics-2020-107193

Vaccine nationalism's politics. D. P. Fidler. *Science*, Vol. 369, Issue 6505. P. 749. DOI: https://doi.org/10.1126/science.abe2275

The Reemergence of Vaccine Nationalism. *Georgetown Journal of International Affairs (online). Saint Louis U. Legal Studies Research Paper No. 2020-16.* Posted : 16 July 2020.

COVID-19 and the cost of vaccine nationalism. M. Hafner et al. *RAND* 2020.

The COVID-19 Vaccine Race: Intellectual Property, Collaborations (s), Nationalism and Misinformation. 64 Wash. U. J. L. & Pol'y 167 (2021).

Global landscape of patents related to human coronaviruses. K. Liu et al. *Int J Bio Sci.* 2021; 17(6): 1588-1599. DOI: https://doi.org/10.7150/ijbs.58807.

Covax must go beyond proportional allocation of covid vaccines to ensure fair and equitable access. L. M. Herzog, E. J. Emanuel, M. S. McCoy. *BMJ* 2021; 372. DOI: https://doi.org/10.1136/bmj.m4853.

Vaccine Hesitancy

> "The claim that vaccines will put selective pressure on the coronavirus and turn into a wild monster is not borne out of science."
>
> – Anonymous

> "I made my tin foil hat from the aluminum in your vaccines."
>
> – Anti vaxxer

> "I think social media is playing a big role in amplifying misinformation, which is leading to people not taking the vaccine, which is killing them."
>
> – Nahid Bhadelia

The reluctance of people to receive safe and effective recommended available vaccines, known as "vaccine hesitancy' was happening prior to the COVID-19 pandemic. Widespread acceptance of vaccines for SARS-CoV-2 is the only alternative in fighting with the ongoing COVID-19 pandemic around the world. However, achieving high uptake by the general population is a real challenge, in part, due to the online misinformation about the vaccines that leads to vaccine hesitancy.

Universal uptake of vaccines and access to vaccine equity require understanding, whether people are willing to be vaccinated, and the underlying reasons, why they are not unwilling to do so, and the most trusted sources of information that have been using for their decision-making. This is important since it is difficult to introduce a vaccine mandate that is primarily against the peoples' privacy, and the right to choose options for their wellbeing.

In September 2020, a RCT was conducted in the UK and the USA to quantify how exposure to online misinformation about COVID-19 vaccines affects intent to get vaccinated .The data suggested that recent misinformation induced a decline in intent 6.2 percentage points (95th percentile interval 3.9 to 8.5) in the UK and 6.4 percentage points (95th percentile interval 4.0 to 8.8) in the USA among those who stated that they would definitely take a vaccine. Also, the study found that some socio-demographic groups were differentially impacted by exposure to misinformation. Importantly, the study was further able to show that scientific-sounding misinformation is more strongly associated with declines in vaccination intent. Among those who are opposed to vaccination (about 15 per cent of the population), many reject any discussion that involves science. Thus it is critical that worldwide biomedical journals must ensure that the use of 'expedited reviews' does not compromise the robustness of the peer-review process of important publications dealing with the safety and efficacy of the vaccines, and related research findings.

The reasons for COVID-19 vaccine acceptance and hesitancy remain complex. The periodic emergence of COVID-19 variants, and rapidly evolving knowledge about the interventions based on new research findings add more to its complexity.

A survey was undertaken between June 2020 and January 2021 across 15 studies carried out in Africa, South Asia, Latin America, Russia, and the United States. The data clearly indicate that vaccine acceptance is explained primarily by emphasizing personal protection against COVID-19, whereas questions about side effects are the critical in their decision-making to be vaccinated.

Following a similar trend, vaccine misinformation and its associated vaccine hesitancy keeps growing in India, as well. Using multiple platforms and tricks to harass moderators (science defenders), anti-vaxxers are spreading rumors about vaccine takers turning impotent or become magnetic after vaccine shots. To beat moderation algorithms, such as FactCheck.org, anti-vaxxers are using words like "CV" instead of coronavirus or "vaax" as opposed to vaccine. Furthermore, they also have backup accounts, so if one gets banned, another pops up.

Scientists in many parts of the world are being harassed online, for advocating true scientific facts, and their support for vaccines. According to Digital Empowerment Foundation, India, which has been running vaccination drives at over 1,000 digital rural centers across the country, the general population believes that government wants to control the population, forcing them to get vaccinated. Also, according to BBC (British Broadcasting Company) news, another widely-shared, but inaccurate claim that compares India favorably over the USA and UK, saying that the vaccine is free in India, while in both the USA and in UK you will pay.

Also, there are some claims, by a specific community that COVID-19 vaccines contain pork, and the consumption of pork products is forbidden for them. Having said that, pork gelatin has sometimes been used as a stabilizer in vaccines for some diseases. However, neither of the two vaccines being rolled out in India, such as Covaxin and Covishield, has such products in them. Additionally, release of a sensational video advocating a miracle cure of COVID-19 disease, by *Gaumutra* (cow urine), began populating nearly all prominent social media channels. The ICMR has issued appeals to the general population not to self-administer medicine.

Thus, one of the India's greatest challenges to mass vaccination is not the logistics or supply chain, rather fake news, misinformation, and the vaccine naysayers. In the end, the world shares a collective responsibility in fighting this ongoing COVID-19 pandemic effectively. It is important that continued research on COVID-19 vaccine acceptance, and hesitancy should be a priority.

Figure 13. Vaccine hesitancy as reflected by the reluctance among the people in getting vaccinated in the USA between February 15, 2021 and September 15, 2021 and in UK between December 15, 2020 and September 15, 2021.

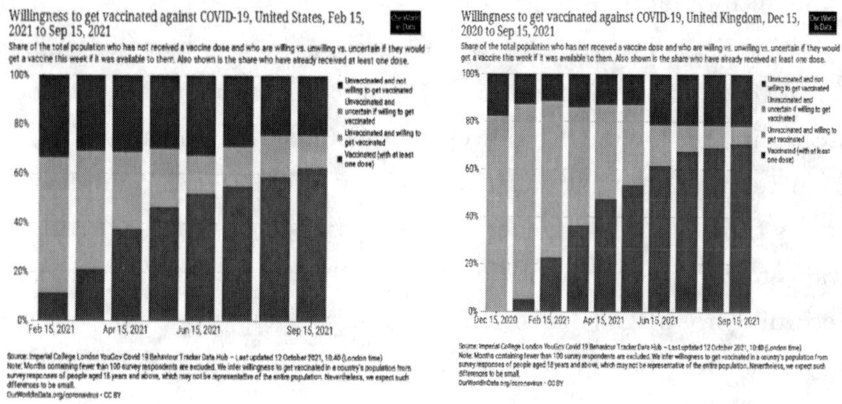

Source: Our World in Data.

Figure 14. The model illustrating how vaccine hesitancy can be influenced by individual behavior influenced by multitude of factors, such as knowledge or past experience.

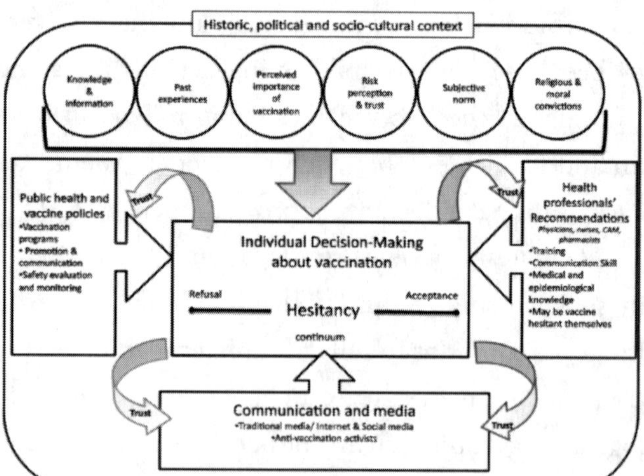

Source: E. Dube et al. https://doi.org/10.4161/hv.24657.

Figure 15. Online trolling and abusive behaviors experienced by the science advocates from the anti-science community.

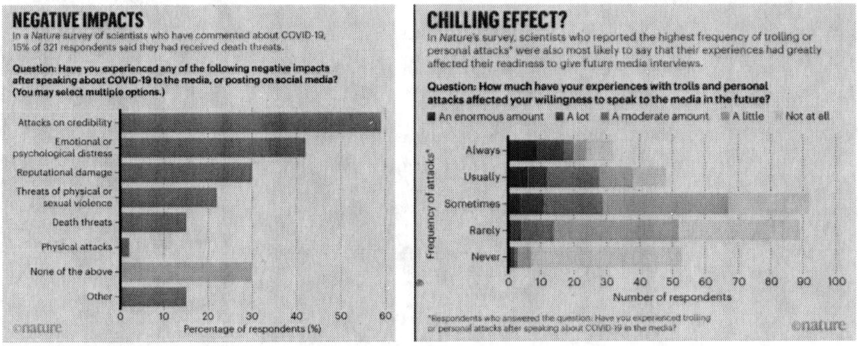

Source: *Nature analysis*

References

COVID-19 vaccine hesitancy can be overcome through relatable stories and accessible information. National Post. https://nationalpost-com.cdn.ampproject.org/c/s/nationalpost.com/pmn/news-pmn/covid-19-vaccine-hesitancy-can-be-overcome-through-relatable-stories-and-accessible-information/wcm/e23d4211-c7c0-4837-b8f5-bd133fc279fc/amp/

Challenges facing COVID-19 vaccination in India: Lessons from the initial vaccine rollout. A. Pandey et al. *Journal of Global Health* 11, 2021. DOI: https://doi.org/10.7189/jogh.11.03083.

Why some people doesn't want a Covid-19 vaccine. https://www.bbc.com/future/article/20210720-the-complexities-of-vaccine-hesitancy.

'For curing coronavirus, global leaders must drink cow urine': Hindu Mahasabha chief. https://www.hindustantimes.com/india-news/for-curing-coronavirus-global-leaders-must-drink-cow-urine-hindu-mahasabha-chief/story-xLvCFC18GU6Q7YYII3v1N.html.

Faith or safety? Covid vaccines spark religious concerns over pork gelatin, cow blood. https://www.indiatoday.in/coronavirus-outbreak/vaccine-updates/story/religious-hurdle-for-covid-19-vaccines-religious-leaders-raise-concern-over-pork-gelatin-cow-blood-in-vaccines-1753992-2020-12-28.

Measuring the impact of COVID-19 misinformation on vaccination intent in the UK and USA. S. Loomba et al. *Nature Human Behavior* 5, 337-348 (2021). DOI: https://doi.org/10.1038/s41562-021-01056-1).

Vaccine hesitancy: Definition, scope and determinants. N. E. MacDonald. *Vaccine.* Vol. 33, Issue 34, 2015, Pages 4161-4164. DOI: https://doi.org/10.1016/j.vaccine.2015.04.036

Understanding COVID-19 vaccine hesitancy. S. Machingaidze & C. S. Wiysonge. *Nature Medicine* 27, 1338-1339 (2021). DOI: https://doi.org/10.1038/s41591-021-01459-7

COVID-19 vaccine acceptance and hesitancy in low-and middle-income countries. J. S. S. Arce et al. *Nature Medicine* 27, 1385-1394 (2021). DOI; https://doi.org/10.1038/s41591-021-01454-y

'I hope you die': how the COVID pandemic unleashed attacks on scientists. https://www.nature.com/articles.d41586-021-02741-x

Vaccine Equity

"Health system leaders reflect on addressing the pandemic, health equity and the intersection of the two."

– David Raths

" No one is safe, until everyone is."

– Anonymous

"And I think we'll be in a position to be able to share vaccines, as well as know-how, with other countries who are in real need. That's the hope and expectation."

– Joe Biden

Vaccine equity is primarily targeted to overcome the pandemic by mitigating the inequalities that lie at the root of numerous global challenges, along with a robust drive for a global recovery, from the worst consequences of the pandemic (W.H.O).

It is often said that 'This virus does not discriminate' by many politicians across the world, to convince people that no one is free of risk, when it comes to contracting SARS-CoV-2. Although, there is no discrimination on the nature of the virus to infect people, there is social discrimination, based on the inequalities deeply embedded within the societal system. For example, people from black, Asian and minority ethnic groups (BAME), and those living in deprived areas, such as slums and homeless people are more likely to be infected by the virus SARS-CoV-2, together with poorer outcomes from the disease. These socioeconomic and ethnic inequalities, in terms of prevalence of infectious disease, and its associated case fatality and mortality rates, have been observed in different health systems, across Europe and America. Thus, for the most disadvantageous communities in the society, COVID-19 is reflected as a syndemic-a co-occurring synergistic pandemic, that interacts with, and is exacerbated by chronic health, and unequal social condition.

Moreover, history suggests that access to good healthcare favor people of higher socioeconomic position as per the *inverse care law*. The more related to it is the *inverse equity hypothesis* that suggests deployments of new healthcare interventions, primarily favor more privileged members of the society, that in turn increases health inequalities, at least, for the short term. Thus, due to this preferential access and uptake, less privileged groups always lag behind their more privileged counterparts.

The COVID-19 2020 pandemic exposed weaknesses and disparities in multiple domains in the society, and widened the gender-based inequalities around the world. Inequalities in getting access to life saving, new healthcare intervention, such as COVID-19 vaccines, is the most deleterious inequality among others. It is driven by the science policy, politics, and social forces that all converge in such a critical moment of the history, the COVID-19 pandemic, to remind us the awesome power of a contagion. The goal for all of us is effectively marshalling the great capacities of STI, vaccine manufacturing, and globalization leading to a vaccine-enabled, easily accessible, and holistic solution in the ongoing battle against COVID-19. If we fail to do so, it is likely, that the global community will be a victim of nationalistic pettiness, intellectual segregation and isolation, and denialism leading to increased global healthcare disparities that in turn, will only heighten the magnitude, and further prolong the duration of this ongoing crisis across the world.

The rapid development of highly effective and broadly safe COVID-19 vaccines is a remarkable feat of STI, and scientifically unprecedented in scope and speed. However, this development has been largely orchestrated by the High-Income Countries (HICs) due to their urgent need, and the ability to channel massive amount of financing in vaccine development, where the COVID-19 disease initially struck especially hard.

The pathway from vaccine development to vaccination is long, and many steps in the trajectory from prioritization of development, setting criteria in designing clinical trials (inclusive of all ethnicities, race, age demographics etc.), licensing, costing, manufacturing, and finally the global distribution have resulted unequal, and delayed across to these across global population. As of April 9, 2021, 40 per cent of the 726 million doses of COVID-19 vaccines administered globally have been in 27 wealthy nations, representing only 11 per cent of the global population. In contrast, people from less-wealthy nations (11%) have been vaccinated only 1.6 per cent of COVID-19 vaccines, till date. This discrepancy in equity, is in part, due to reported higher burden of COVID-19 disease in some rich countries-likely due to an aging population leading to high case fatality and mortality rates as opposed to less-resourced countries with larger young population, such as India. The limited vaccine availability in Low-to-Middle-Income (LMIC) countries is exemplified by the inability of vaccinating even the most high-risk populations, such as healthcare workers and older adults with comorbidities, comprising 1-10% of the population, as estimated by the W.H.O. While LMICs are struggling to procure enough doses of vaccines, some HICs have started vaccinating less vulnerable younger people. Furthermore, for future needs, these countries have secured enough vaccine doses, and manufacturing capacity to vaccinate their population several times over (booster doses).

The definition of vaccine equity arises from a model known as the "*health capability paradigm*" that is primarily used to define health equity. This tells us how health equity can be constructed based on three principals. First, the principal of *equality*: are vaccines outside and within countries allocated equally to ensure population coverage indiscriminately? Second, the *prioritarian* principle: this justifies the allocation of vaccines to the hardest-hit population, even depriving all others who are affected marginally due to pandemic disease. Thus, essentially, this principle aims to improve the situation of the most deprived, and affected population in the world. Third, the principle of the *threshold* view: this states that international allocation of vaccine resources is based on minimally adequate health status. The combination of all three aspects gives rise to the theory "*shortfall equality*". It primarily measures the extent to which certain individuals, and populations fall short of target levels. Moreover, it is an effective approach to equality assessment, accounting for variation when assessing health capabilities, and health achievements of different individuals and populations. This approach sets a threshold of health norm against which measurement in gaps in health for certain individuals and populations is done.

Also, the healthcare equity analysis is driven by the application of Tanahashi model of health service that can be adapted to vaccination coverage in the population across the world. The model has six different components-First, *applicability*: inequality of access to diagnostics and poorly developed disease surveillance will result inaccurate estimation of disease burden, and identifying risk groups that challenge articulation of needs. Second, *appropriateness*: is the vaccine appropriately designed for the national context? For example, the expensive cold-chain requirements and use of multiple vaccine doses will require complex vaccine administration and logistics. Third, *availability*: are there sufficient vaccine doses available for an effective vaccine rollout? Also, are there trained and decently paid health workers to conduct a vaccination program? Fourth, *affordability*: are vaccines affordable considering beneficiary government health expenditure and fiscal limitations in safeguarding other essential health services? Fifth, *acceptability*: are vaccines trusted by the population, and whether the government has adequate communication strategies promoting vaccination and mitigating the vaccine misinformation, and hesitancy in the population? Lastly, *efficacy and effectiveness*: Are vaccines safe and effective? Are regulatory authorities equipped with the ability to exercise liability practices that are needed in case of serious vaccine side effects? Taken together, to have an equitable coverage of world's population for vaccination, it is important to invest in vaccine delivery strategies that generate demand, allocate and distribute vaccines, and verify coverage. In order to achieve all these targets, commitment to periodic engagement with communities for vaccine advocacy, political will to ensure the cooperation of local and national governments, efficient vaccine distribution through supply chains, and finally real-time vaccination tracking systems must be identified to verify vaccine coverage in the population

The ethics of fair allocation of vaccines and global solidarity entrust HICs to allocate a share of these for other countries who have less ability to manufacture sufficient doses of vaccine to immunize its population due to economic reason. This has resulted the expansion of the W.H.O-supported COVAX initiative co-led by Gavi, the Vaccine Alliance, and Coalition for Epidemic Preparedness Innovations (CEPI) and the W.H.O. In spite of this initiative, the supply of vaccines and access for many developing countries is unclear to date, due to very low levels of coverage achieved. Furthermore, vaccine nationalism has emerged as a big threat in facilitating global cooperation for achieving vaccine equity. For example, the decision by the U.S. government to ban export of critical raw materials needed for vaccine manufacturing in other countries has affected the supply chains necessary to augment vaccine supply in LMIC. In order to achieve vaccine-induced herd immunity, about 70-90% of the population needs to be vaccinated, assuming about 80 per cent vaccine efficacy and R_0 (reproduction number) between 2.5 to 3.5. Thus, any delay in achieving uniform vaccine equity across the population in a country, due to lack of robust domestic vaccine manufacturing, and deployment capacity, are likely to affect severely the management of pandemic. This has worst consequences in terms of lives lost due to COVID-19 and non-COVID complications, as a result of more focus on COVID-19 disease and neglecting non-COVID-19 diseases, a multitude of public health problems, the continuing increased costs of hospitalization and treatment, and the deleterious effects on economy from school and workplace closures, that in turn, severely affect academic services and industrial outputs.

Prior to the development of COVID-19 vaccines, a cocktail of powerful antiviral dugs revolutionized HIV treatment in the Western world in 1996, saving numerous lives. However, it took seven years for the drugs to be available in the hardest hit continent, the Africa. In another instance, during the 2009 HIN1 influenza pandemic, the USA and many European countries donated 10 per cent of their vaccine stocks to poorer countries only after reserving enough stock for their own populations. Thus, a global initiative such as COVAX is helpful in terms of securing new vaccines by LMICs as soon as these are developed, and as backups, in case the vaccine manufactured by a country has failed to meet the desired efficacy. However, a country is allowed to access only certain fraction of the vaccine doses through COVAX that cover only 20 per cent of its population. So, a really big international effort is needed by involving United Nations or the G-20 to boost vaccine equity across the world in a timely manner. Without this, it is unlikely the vaccine doses will reach to those who need these more. The slow process in attaining vaccine equity will only enhance inadequacy in getting most of the population vaccinated, resulting unnecessary deaths.

Although, vaccine nationalism is good way to protect its population from the shortage of vaccine doses, just a few days after starting its own COVID-19 vaccination program, India helped few underdeveloped countries in providing the indigenous vaccines as grant-in-aid. This was in contrary to some HICs who stockpiled vaccines, and denied to remove the IP rights in World Trade Organization (WTO). India's initial grant-in-aid to other countries resulted a deep humanitarian crisis in the nation, and adversely affected vaccination rates at the peak of the second wave of COVID-19 pandemic in India.

Historically, equity always enables maximizing benefits from limited resources. India's original vaccination strategy is to sequentially vaccinate priority groups, such as healthcare workers, frontline workers, people with more than 50 years of age, and younger people with comorbidities, such as diabetes, hypertension, cancer, and lung diseases. Thus, in principle, this vaccination strategy invokes equity-prioritizing those at highest risk. However, during the worst second wave of COVID-19 pandemic, Government of India announced a "liberal policy" for vaccination. In midst of worst crisis in the month of April 2021, when the nation already being riddled with acute shortages of vaccine doses together with astoundingly high mortality rates, an universal vaccination strategy among adults who are higher than 18 years of old, further aggravated the difficulty in achieving vaccine equity.

Moreover, to enforce vaccine manufactures' for making more doses of vaccines at a rapid pace, the government effectively removed price controls for manufacturers. This is unusual as no other federal democracy is making citizens to pay for COVID-19 vaccines or have states competing to secure supplies. This has resulted vaccine manufacturers resorted to differential and predatory pricing due to huge demand amid all the deaths and despair in the second wave of COVID-19 pandemic. The Government of India fixed prices for state governments that are almost twice of the price paid by the union government and it is four times for private hospital. The "liberal policy" also induces regional inequalities as richer state governments will have the capacity to buy more vaccine doses for non-priority groups while states with poor revenues and weaker health system will have to wait longer for buying vaccines for priority groups. Thus, adopting a "One Nation-One Price-One Vaccine Buyer" policy that allows Government of India buys and makes it free for all Indian citizens is the need of the hours. The good news is, of late, Government of India has started providing vaccines to all of the Indian citizens for free of cost.

Additionally, vaccine-patent waivers by WTO can be of great help in equitable distribution of COVID-19 vaccines across the world. However, the narrow geography of the global vaccine-making chain can result in imbalance in vaccine distribution. Nevertheless, the waivers would enable countries, such as India with strong vaccine-making capacities, to churn out large quantities. Although, it is possible that waiving IP/patent protection might not speed up and/or scale up manufacturing and distribution of the vaccines, as the primary reason behind the delays in scaling up vaccine manufacturing capability is raw material shortage, and inadequate GMP (good manufacturing practice) certified sophisticated manufacturing facilities in many countries.

Another concern is that vaccines are biologics that require extremely complex manufacturing process, unlike small-molecule medicines, such as Aspirin are made through chemical processes. Since biologics are large complex molecules, it is often difficult to reverse engineer these, and launch their generic versions (called biosimilars) in the market. Thus, waiving the IP right does not always guarantee a smooth transition of biologics for commercialization due to minimal effect of IP waiver on the drug approval regulatory process. Additionally, the proposed IP waiver in WTO faced serious opposition within the HICs. Thus, it would be unrealistic to witness a major change in terms of accessibility or affordability to vaccine. Thus, it needs a diligent effort to convert an illusive dream "vaccine equity" into a realistic proposition.

Taken together, a comprehensive understanding of vaccine equity, its challenges, and importance in the society that includes policy leaders, will accelerate the uniform vaccine distribution to the entire world population with ease by overcoming vaccine hesitancy and nationalism, imperialism, geopolitics, and effectively end the current pandemic. This will allow global citizens to focus on other important long-term challenges of our time, such as food insecurity, poverty, decent work, population health, economic growth, and other priorities, that are listed under SDGs.

Figure 16. COVAX and financialization of global vaccine equity: Distribution of COVAX into buyers' and distribution clubs.

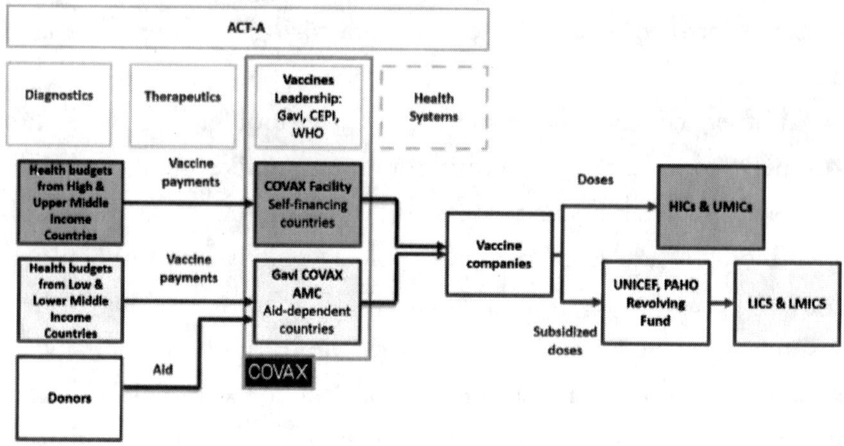

Source: F. Sten, *Global Health* 17, 112 (2021).

References

Learning from past mistakes? The COVID-19 vaccine and the inverse equity hypothesis. A. Todd and C. Bambra. *European Journal of Public Health,* Volume 31, Issue 1, February 2021. P2. DOI: https://doi.org/10.1093/eurpub/chaa243.

COVID-19 Pandemic and health inequalities. Bambra C et al. *J Epidemiol Community Health* 2020; 74: 964-68. DOI: https://doi.org/10.1136/jech-2020-214401.

The Inverse care law. J. T. Hart. *The Lancet* Vol. 297, Issue 7696, P405-412, 1971. DOI: https://doi.org/10.1016/S0140-6736(71)92410-X.

Explaining trends in inequalities: evidence from Brazilian child health studies. C. G. Victoria et al. *Lancet* 2000; Sep 23; 356:1093-8. DOI: https://doi.org/10.1016/S0140-6736(00)02741-0.

SARS-CoV-2 vaccine development, access, and equity. J. H. Kim. *J Exp Med* (2020) 217 (11): e20201288. DOI: https://doi.org/10.1084/jem.20201288.

Randall T. The World's Wealthiest Countries Are Getting Vaccinated 25 Times Faster: Bloomberg Equality: 2021. https://www.bloomberg.com/news/articles/2021-04-09/when-will-world-be-fully-vaccinated-pace-is-2-400-faster-in-wealthy-countries).

WHO SAGE Roadmap for prioritizing the use of COVID-19 vaccines in the context of limited supply. 2020. https://www.who.int/docs/default-source/immunization/sage/covid/sage-prioritization-roadmap-covid19 vaccines.pdf.

Global Health Justice. J.P. Ruger. *Public Health Ethics.* 2009; 2(3): 261-275. DOI: https://doi.org/10.1093/phe/php019.

Ethics and governance of global health inequalities. J.P. Ruger. *J Epidemiol Community Health* 2006, 60(11): 998-1002. DOI: https://doi.org/10.1136/jech.2005.041947.

Healthcare equity analysis: applying the Tanahashi model of health service coverage to community health systems following devolution in Kenya. R. McCollum et al. *International Journal for Equity in Health* 18:65 (2019). DOI: https://doi.org/10.1186/s12939-019-0967-5.

COVID-19 Vaccine to Vaccination: Why Leaders Must Invest In Delivery Strategies Now. L.W. Rebecca et al. *Health Affairs.* Vol. 40 No.1, 2020. DOI: https://doi.org/10.1377/hlthaff.2020.01523.

Reserving coronavirus disease 2019 vaccines for global access: cross sectional analysis. A.D. So et al *BMJ.* 2020; 371:m4750. DOI: https://doi.org/10.1136/bmj.m4750.

https://ourworldindata.org/grapher/cumulative-covid-vaccinations

The Economist. American export controls threaten to hinder global vaccine production. April 24, 2021. https://www.economist.com/science-and-technology/2021/04/22/american-export-controls-threaten-to-hinder-global-vaccine-production?

Ethical Considerations and Challenges During the COVID-19 Vaccine Deployment: Experiences from an Indian Perspectives. S. Basu and S. Mishra. *Vaccine research.* 7(2): 56-60, 2020. DOI: https://doi.org/10.52547/vacres.7.2.56).

https://science.sciencemag.org/content/sci/369/6503/489.full.pdf

Vaccine Efficacy Needed for a COVID-19 Coronavirus Vaccine to Prevent or Stop an Epidemic as the Sole Intervention. S.M. Bartach. *Am J Prev Med.* 2020 Oct; 59(4): 493-503. DOI: https://doi.org/10.1016/j.amepre.2020.06.011.

Ministry of External Affairs. Made-in-India COVID19 vaccine supplies so far (in lakhs): Ministry of External Affairs, Government of India: 2021. https://www.mea.gov.in/vaccine-supply.htm.

Priorities for the COVID-19 pandemic at the start of 2021: statement of the Lancet COVID-19 commission. J.D. Sachs et al. *Lancet* 2021 Mar 13: 397(10278): 947-950. DOI: https://doi.org/10.1016/S0140-6736(21)00388-3.

MOHFW-GOI. COVID-19 vaccines: operational guidelines New Delhi: Ministry of Health & Family Welfare, Government of India. https://www.mogfw.gov.in/pdf/COVID19VaccineOG111Chapter16.pdf.

New "liberal" policy: States to spend a tidy sum for vaccination drive. P. Sahu. Financial Express; 2021. https://www.financialexpress.com/economy/new-liberal-policy-states-to-spend-a-tidy-sum-for-vaccination-drive/2237743).

"Don't Leave Vaccine Pricing and Distribution To Manufactures": Supreme Court Questions Centre's COVID Vaccination Policy 2021. J. Mahaj https://www.livelaw.in/top-stories/supreme-court-questions-centres-vaccine-policy-vaccine-pricing-and-distribution-manufacturers-173389.

The Chronological Evolution of Vaccine Types, and Technology Platforms

"It's important for children to be vaccinated so that they have the opportunity to become adults."

– Brad McKay

"A once-dismissed idea became a leading technology in the Covid vaccine race: The story of mRNA."

– Damian Grade

"India's DNA COVID vaccine is a world first-more are coming."

– Nature

Scientific research over many years has led to the development of a large number of vaccines that elicit effective humoral and cellular immune responses to protect individuals against infection. In spite of lots of early success, researchers continue to investigate new vaccine strategies for the prevention of existing, and emerging infectious diseases. Major advances in understanding the underlying fundamental mechanisms of complex biological interactions between the invading pathogens, and their human hosts have facilitated the further development of vaccines. Apart from these valuable insights, significant advances in laboratory techniques, and technologies have additionally boosted the development of new types of vaccines.

Vaccines are broadly classified into 3 types: Whole-pathogen vaccines, subunit vaccines, and nucleic acid vaccines. Each type is designed to train the immune system how to fight effectively against the infectious agent, and to combat the severity of the disease, as a result of the infection. The factors that are most important in designing, and the development of a vaccine are how the immune system responds to the infectious agent, who needs to be vaccinated, and the best technology platform(s) or approaches that will be used to develop the vaccine.

Whole-pathogen vaccines

Traditional vaccines consist of whole pathogens that have been either killed or weakened so that they cannot cause disease when administered into individuals.

The first human vaccines against viruses were based using weaker or attenuated forms of viruses to generate immunity. The smallpox vaccine used cowpox, a poxvirus that was similar to smallpox to generate immune response against smallpox, but did not cause serious illness to the vaccinated individuals. Rabies was the first virus attenuated in the laboratory settings to create a vaccine for humans.

The major advantage of using whole-pathogen vaccines is their ability to generate strong immune responses in the body. Among whole-pathogen vaccines, the inactivated vaccines use the killed version of the pathogen that causes a disease. However, since a pathogen used to make inactivated vaccine does not replicate in the host body, it requires repeated doses for an effective immunity to be achieved. The first dose is the one that prepares the immune system to respond, but a protective immune response does not develop until the second, and subsequent booster doses. Also, inactivated vaccines produce immune responses in different ways than, live, attenuated whole pathogen vaccines. This explains why multiple doses are necessary to build up and/or maintain long-lasting immunity. The inactivated polio vaccine is an example of this type of vaccine.

Typically, all inactivated whole-pathogen vaccines follow a similar manufacturing protocol in which the pathogen is first grown on a substrate in the laboratory setting to produce large quantities of antigens. Historically, vaccine manufacturers have been using primary cells, tissues, and fertilized eggs as substrates for making large amounts of the whole pathogen. However, of late, manufacturers are increasing inclined toward pathogen growth on continuous cell lines that has resulted cost-effective production, increased vaccine safety, and relatively straightforward up scaling. After the propagation of the pathogen, it is purified and concentrated prior to inactivation. A multitude of well-established inactivation agents and methodologies have been described in the literatures to successfully inactivate whole pathogen for vaccine purposes. Some of the examples are ethylenimine derivatives, ascorbic acid, hydrogen peroxide, UV treatment, heat, and gamma irradiation. Among all of these, only formaldehyde and Beta-Propiolactone (BPL) are widely used for inactivation of licensed human vaccine over many decades.

In most cases, inactivated whole-pathogen vaccines do not cause disease when administered into the individuals. However, the Cutter incident in 1955 was one of the worst pharmaceutical disasters in the world history. In this case, about 380,000 doses of inactivated poliovirus vaccine (IPV), produced at Cutter laboratory, USA, administered into healthy children. In spite of the inactivation process, these vaccine doses contained replication competent poliovirus, due to inadequate purification of the virus during production. As a result of which, 40,000 children who received the vaccine had abortive poliomyelitis, 51 were permanently paralyzed, and 5 died.

Furthermore, clinical trials with a formalin-inactivated respiratory syncytical virus (RSV) when introduced into the naïve infants had shown disastrous outcome. About 80 per cent of the vaccine takers were hospitalized due to circulating RSV as compared to hospitalization of only 5 per cent in the control vaccine group. Also, the vaccine had failed to protect the disease. Two vaccine recipients died due to vaccine-induced disease. Upon investigation, the deaths were found to be due to an unfavorable immune response, as a result of skewed Th2 (a subtype of T-helper cells), and the absence of affinity maturation of the antibody generated against the antigen contained in the vaccine. In addition, a large fraction of vaccine-induced antibodies were directed to non-protective epitopes, as formalin treatment used for inactivating the whole virus had altered the key epitopes that were required to produce neutralizing antibodies for protection against the disease.

A formalin-inactivated measles vaccine was licensed in 1963, but, unfortunately, resulted in a similar outcome. The vaccine was able to produce neutralizing antibodies in the vaccinated individuals, however, immune protection waned rapidly, and recipients developed susceptibility toward measles. Importantly, when they were re-infected due to breakthrough infections, a more severe, atypical measles developed due to lack of cytotoxic T cell response, and low affinity antibodies that were attributed to formaldehyde-induced changes of the measles F protein during inactivation. Moreover, reversion to virulent viruses, and resulting transmission of the disease have been observed frequently in the past with the inactivated poliovirus vaccine, yellow fever, and rotavirus.

In contrast, live vaccines use a weakened (or attenuated) version of the pathogen that causes a disease. Advances in the tissue culture techniques in the 1950s resulted development of live-attenuated vaccines. The measles, mumps and rubella (MMR) are one of the examples. This type of vaccines elicits robust and long-lasting immune protection against development of disease, as they are very similar to the natural infectious agent. In most cases, one or two doses of most live vaccines can give individuals a lifetime of protection against a pathogen, and the disease it causes.

Typically, live vaccines are made in such a way that the pathogen is not able to cause disease itself, but can produce a robust immune response, as opposed to dead or inactivated vaccines. Since they are being attenuated, they are unable to replicate in the host to the same extent as live unaltered viruses, that means they lose the ability to infect the host to a great extent, but good enough for the host to develop robust, and long-lasting immunity. Live vaccines are derived from "wild," or disease-causing, viruses or bacteria. These wild pathogens are attenuated, or weakened, in a laboratory, usually by repeated culturing. The measles virus used as a vaccine today, was initially isolated from a child with measles disease in 1954. After a decade of serial passage using tissue culture technique, the wild virus was transformed into attenuated vaccine virus.

Although, live-attenuated virus used as vaccine can produce a robust immune response in the body, sometimes, it may cause fatal reactions, as a result of uncontrolled replication (growth) of the vaccine virus. This typically happens in persons suffering from immunodeficiency disorders, due to leukemia, treatment with some immunosuppressive drugs, or human immunodeficiency virus (HIV) infection. Moreover, a live attenuated vaccine virus could revert to its original pathogenic form. This is known to happen only with live (oral) polio vaccine. Also, it is possible that robust immunity from a live attenuated vaccine virus may not develop due to interference from circulating antibodies in the individuals against the vaccine vector virus.

Furthermore, antibody introduced into the body due to transplacental source, or transfusion, can potentially interfere with the replication of the vaccine organism, leading to poor and/ or negligible immune response to the vaccine, that is known as vaccine failure. In addition, live attenuated vaccines are fragile, and can be easily destroyed by the heat and light. Thus, they must be handled and stored carefully. Some examples of live-attenuated vaccines are MMR, rotavirus, smallpox, chickenpox, and yellow fever.

Additionally, modern genetic engineering techniques have enabled creation of chimeric viruses, which contain genetic information from and exhibit biological properties of different parent viruses. Interestingly, NIAID (National Institute of Allergy and Infectious Disease, USA) has developed live-attenuated chimeric vaccine backbone with Zika virus surface protein, is currently undergoing early-stage testing to determine its safety and efficacy, to be used as live-attenuated vaccine virus.

Subunit vaccines

In contrast to whole-cell vaccine in which the entire pathogen is introduced into the recipient to induce immune responses, subunit vaccines include only the key components, or antigens, that robustly induce the immune responses.

The advantage of using only the essential antigen in a subunit vaccine is minimal adverse effects, as exemplified by the development of a new generation of pertussis (whooping cough) vaccines. The first pertussis vaccines, introduced in the 1940s, consisted of inactivated *Bordetella pertussis* bacteria. Due to many adverse effects of the whole-cell pertussis vaccines, people used to avoid the vaccines that resulted a significant increase in new infections in the 1970s.

Fundamental research at NIAID, USA, and elsewhere, led to the development of acellular pertussis vaccines by purifying individual *B. pertussis* components. These vaccines are equally effective as whole-cell vaccines with minor adverse effects. However, often, the synthetic subunit vaccines are not devoid of lower immunogenicity compared to live attenuated vaccines.

Polysaccharide vaccines are a unique type of inactivated subunit vaccine, composed of long chains of sugar molecules that constitute the surface capsule of certain bacteria. The first licensed vaccine against *Haemophilus influenza* type B (Hib) was a polysaccharide vaccine. However, its usefulness was limited, as it did not produce robust immune responses in infants-the age group with the highest prevalence of Hib disease. To overcome this, a conjugate vaccine was made, in which the Hib polysaccharide "conjugated" to a protein antigen to augment its efficiency of disease protection. This formulation greatly increased the ability of the young children to resist Hib infection. Subsequently, conjugate vaccines were made against pneumococcal and meningococcal disease. Other vaccines against bacterial illness, such as diphtheria and tetanus vaccines, aim to elicit immune responses against disease-causing proteins, known as toxins, secreted by the bacteria. The antigens in these toxoid vaccines are chemically inactivated toxins (toxoids). They create immunity to the parts of the pathogen that cause a disease, instead of the whole pathogen itself.

In the 1980s, with the invention of recombinant DNA technology, it was effectively utilized to develop the first recombinant protein vaccine: the hepatitis B vaccine. The antigen (HBsAg) used to develop vaccine was made in yeast cells into which the genetic code of HBsAg had been inserted.

Since the beginning of the recombinant DNA technology, various protein production technologies have been developed that are efficient, relatively inexpensive, allowing cost-effective production of recombinant proteins in microbial (such as *Escherichia coli*) and other expression host system systems, such as yeasts, mammalian cell culture expression, and insect cells. Several vaccine antigens have been produced in *E. coli*, including, in 1998, an FDA approved Lyme disease vaccine that contained recombinantly-expressed outer surface lipoprotein, OspA, from *Borrelia burgdorferi*. Other examples of *E. coli* produced antigens include vaccines against meningococcal serogroup B infections, developed by Pfizer that uses two variants of the meningococcal factor H-binding protein (fHBP) as antigens. Bexsero, a vaccine developed by GSK, uses 3 immunogenic meningococcal antigens (fHbp, NadA, and NHBA) made in *E. coli.*

However, *E. coli* expression system does not provide post-translational modifications (PTMs), such as glycosylation that can affect the ability of the vaccine antigen to produce robust immune responses in the individuals due to its improper protein folding. PTMs also affect the protein characteristics, such as solubility, bioavailability, pharmacokinetics, and overall stability of the protein antigen. Thus it is critical that protein antigen has to be made in the expression system that confers correct folding, and disulfide bond formation rendering it to be functionally active. Yeasts are another well-known microbial expression platform. Unlike, *E. coli*, yeasts often allows secreting recombinant proteins in extracellular spaces, which makes the downstream purification process simpler, and less expensive. The correct PTMs in this lower eukaryotic expression system, results proper folding of the recombinant proteins to be functional. Apart from recombinant hepatitis B surface antigens (HBsAg) expressed in yeast, another licensed vaccine, Gardsil, uses the major capsid protein, L1, from the HPVL1 as its antigen.

Furthermore, though, more costly, mammalian expression systems are attractive in the sense that glycoprotein antigens retain their native structure and PTMs, constituting the majority of the recently approved biologics. An example of this type of vaccines is Shingrix, the herpes zoster vaccine manufactured by a pharmaceutical giant Glaxo Smith Kline (GSK), by using Chinese Hamster Ovary (CHO) cells to produce recombinant glycoprotein E as vaccine antigen.

In addition, insect cells are among the popular choice of recombinant protein expression system for the production of vaccines. COVID-19 subunit vaccine candidates, such as from Novavax, Safoni and Adimmune are produced in a system that uses a baculovirus vector that incorporate the genetic instruction to produce vaccine antigen in insect cells as hosts. To date, there are two licensed vaccines in the USA, that use insect cell expression system; Cervarix and HPV vaccine that uses the recombinant HPVL1 antigen and Flublok, an influenza vaccine using a trivalent hemagglutinin antigen respectively. Moreover, similar to mammalian expression systems, recombinant proteins made in insect cells are well folded, soluble, and contain the desired PTMs. However, N-glycosylation by baculovirus-infected insect cells is not equivalent to those made in higher eukaryotes, such as mammalian expression systems.

Vaccines to protect individuals from HPV infection also are based on recombinant protein antigen. In the early 1990s, scientists discovered that proteins from the outer shell of HPV form particles that closely mimic the virus. These virus-like particles (VLPs) elicit an immune response similar to natural virus. But, VLPs are non infectious, as they do not contain the genetic material the virus needs to replicate inside host cells. Additionally, researchers at NIH, USA, have designed an experimental VLP vaccine that can prevent individuals from getting chikungunya infections.

Furthermore, in an effort to develop a universal flu vaccine, researchers have designed an experimental vaccine using protein ferritin, which can self-assemble into microscopic pieces, known as nanoparticles that display vaccine flu antigen. The nanoparticle-based technology is being further assessed as a technology platform for development of vaccines against MERS coronavirus, RSV, and Epstein Barr virus.

Other subunit vaccine technology platform includes antigen designing based on atomic structure of the proteins. For example, the three-dimensional structure of a protein on the RSV surface, bound to an antibody, lets researchers to identify a key area of the protein that is sensitive to neutralizing antibodies. Subsequently, this knowledge has helped them to modify the RSV protein to stabilize the structural form in which it displays the neutralization-sensitive sites.

Finally, the lower immunogenicity of synthetic subunit vaccine antigens, compared to live attenuated vaccines, is being investigated with improved vaccine carriers. Research over many years indicates that physiochemical properties of these carriers can be modified to confer optimal vaccine antigen presentation, endosomal escape, particle bio-distribution, and cellular trafficking. Also, the carriers can be modified with antigens and ligands to be better targeted to antigen presenting cells, such as dendritic cells to elicit a robust humoral immune responses. These carriers can also be modified with adjuvant to improve cellular, and humoral immune response against the vaccine antigen.

Nucleic Acid Vaccines

Nucleic acid vaccination approach involves introducing genetic material encoding the antigen against which an immune response is anticipated, and desirable. Upon introduction, bodies own cells use this genetic material to produce the vaccine antigens. Administration of nucleic acid vaccines results in the production of viral proteins endogenously, using host's protein synthesis machinery, with native conformation as they have the correct glycosylation profiles, and other

PTMs that accurately mirror the native antigens, produced during natural viral infection. This vaccination approach produces broad long-term immune responses by inducing antibody and cytotoxic T-lymphocytes-mediated immunity to diverse protein antigens.

In the 1990s, researchers found that injection of 'naked' plasmid DNA without any associated lipid, protein or carbohydrate, could elicit immune response. There are several reasons why naked nucleic acids are attractive candidate vectors for many infectious diseases. They are relatively easy to generate, and safe to administer. In contrast to whole-cell pathogen vaccines, nucleic acid vaccines contain only DNA or RNA that is taken up by the host cells, and translated into protein. Moreover, the lack of a viral coat eliminates the possibility, that immune response to the coat of live attenuated virus will be immunodominant over immune responses to the desired transgene antigen. When plasmid DNA is introduced into the body, the antigens that are encoded by the nucleic acid vaccines, captured by the most powerful antigen presenting cells (APCs), dendritic cells (DCs). They acquire antigen by three primary routes. First, DCs can be directly transfected with nucleic acid vaccines. Second, soluble antigen from interstitial spaces secreted, and released by the transfected cells, taken up by the DCs. Third, DCs preferentially take up cells that are injured or killed, as a result of the vaccine, or its function. APCs subsequently present the antigens to B-cell lymphocytes that make antibodies. However, as opposed to whole-cell vaccines, that contains surface molecules, such as lipopolysaccharide (LPS), and a large variety of soluble factors that function as adjuvant, and improve immune responses in the body, the potency of the genetic vaccines can be significantly enhanced by mimicking these signals with adjuvants, such as monophosphoryl lipid A (MPL). NIAID's Vaccine Research Center has developed candidate DNA vaccines to control several viral disease threats during outbreaks, including SARS coronavirus in 2003, H5N1 avian influenza in 2005, HIN1 pandemic influenza in 2009, and Zika virus in 2016.

Instead of delivering DNA or mRNA directly to cells, some vaccines use a harmless virus or bacterium as a vector, or carrier of the vaccine antigen(s). Thus, viral vectors are promising tools for gene therapy, and vaccine development. They can enhance immunogenicity of the vaccine antigen without an adjuvant, and induce a robust cytotoxic T lymphocyte (CTL) response to kill virus-infected cells.

Over the last several decades, many types of viruses have been developed as vaccine vectors. To date, both successful and unsuccessful results have been reported in many clinical trials. The advantages of viral vectors are as follows: (a) highly efficient gene transduction; (b) targeted delivery of genes to specific cell types; and (c) induction of robust cellular and humoral immunity. In contrast to subunit vaccines, that typically prevent infectious disease by eliciting a potent humoral response, recombinant viral vectors enable intracellular antigen expression, and induce a potent CTL response, eliminating virus-infected cells, in addition to generating a strong antibody-mediated immune protection.

However, they are not without disadvantages. In some vectors, stable expression of viral gene into the host genome is achieved via viral integration mechanisms. Jesse Gelsinger, who had undergone adenovirus mediated gene therapy to cure OTCD (ornithine transcarbamylase deficiency syndrome) at the University of Pennsylvania hospital, died due to a fatal immune response triggered by the adenovirus vector. Another obstacle to the clinical use of viral vectors is the presence of pre-existing immunity against the vector that is caused by prior exposure to the virus, and the production of neutralizing antibodies against the vector virus that reduce vaccine efficacy.

Furthermore, the development of viral vectors demands a high biological safety level in order to gain public acceptance. Thus, non- or weekly pathogenic viruses are selected for vaccine development. In most cases, viruses are genetically engineered to eliminate pathogencity. Many of them are replication incompetent. For example, in adenovirus-based vectors, the E1A and E1B encoding regions, which are needed for the replication of the virus, inside the infected-host cells, are deleted, and replaced with target, such as vaccine gene.

The recombinant adenovirus vectors are widely used among other viral vectors, because of their high transduction efficiency, high level of transgene expression, and broad range of viral tropism. Furthermore, they can infect both dividing and non-dividing cells. Researchers around the world are developing and evaluating other recombinant vectored vaccines to protect humans from viruses such as HIV, Zika virus, and Ebola virus. To date, several different viruses have been used as vectors, such as influenza, vesicular stomatitis virus (VSV), measles virus, and adenovirus, which cause common cold in humans. Viral vector vaccines are currently being used to protect individuals from getting COVID-19 disease.

The mRNA vaccines represent a promising alternative to conventional vaccine approach due to their high potency, fast-paced development time, low-cost manufacturing process, due to high yields of *in vitro* transcription reaction, enough to develop vaccines, and safe administration to the vaccine takers. Another advantage of using mRNA vaccines is the safety issue, as mRNA is a non-infectious, non-integrating platform, where genomic integration is a rare phenomenon, and there is no potential risk of infection or insertional mutagenesis, that may be a caveat with DNA-vaccines. Moreover, mRNA has a short half-life, as it degrades quickly inside the body that can be regulated using various modifications, and delivery methods.

The immunogenicity of the mRNA can be down modulated to further increase its safety. The various modifications make mRNA used as vaccine, more stable, and easily translatable to produce fully functional vaccine protein (antigen). Also, mRNA can be easily encapsulated in carrier vesicle, such as lipid membrane that allows it to be taken up by the host cells easily and efficiently, and expressing it abundantly in the cytoplasm where synthesis of vaccine antigen takes place. Since mRNA is the minimal genetic vector, the anti-vector immunity is significantly avoided, that allows it to be administered repeatedly into the body, when needed. As of now, mRNA vaccines are among the most popular ones, used to protect people against COVID-19 disease.

Development of COVID-19 vaccine platforms

A vaccine platform is a 'plug-and-play' technology framework that can be effectively used for any emerging infectious diseases, such as COVID-19. Vaccine platforms use a base carrier or "vehicle," such as nucleic acid, viral vector, or liposome that can be used to develop vaccines for a multitude of infectious and/or non-infectious diseases. The advantage of platform technologies is once a particular technology platform is used to produce one vaccine, the development of future vaccines, using the same platform, would only require substituting the desired antigenic component that normally triggers an effective immune response against the disease. This feature accelerates the speed of vaccine development in a cost-effective manner, streamlines regulatory approval, and mass production.

The worldwide vaccine development effort in response to the ongoing COVID-19 pandemic has been unprecedented in terms of scale and speed. However, historically, vaccine development has always been a lengthy and expensive process prior to the development of COVID-19 vaccines. This is, in part, due to high cost burden, and failure rates that has made development to follow sequence of phases, with multiple pauses required for interim data analyses, need to deal with live potentially hazardous viruses, assessment of safety profile, and the manufacturing decisions. Four major factors have shortened the COVID-19 vaccine development time, such as fast-paced knowledge about the new disease, the technology platforms, and monetary investments; both public and private, and expedited review of the vaccines development by the regulatory bodies worldwide. Importantly, there was prior knowledge about the coronaviruses from work on SARS and MERS that has led scientific community to identify SARS-CoV-2 and massive international collaborations facilitated data sharing among investigators, and in the public domain. A joint EMA/FDA (Emergency Management Agency/Food and Drug Administration) pandemic preparedness-working group was previously established in 2003, which meant major strategies were already in shape. In addition, regulatory bodies have diverted their key resources to expedite review processes that significantly reduce the timelines for the evaluation, and authorization of medicines (EMA and FDA).

At the present moment, there are multiple technology platforms in use for vaccine development, some of which are actively utilized in the production of licensed vaccines. Other approaches are more novel, and yet to be approved for use, but are currently being investigated, as part of the global COVID-19 vaccine development response.

In the case of the inactivated and live-attenuated vaccines, the use of whole virus provides all the viral proteins, lipids, and nucleic acids for immune stimulation, making them highly immunogenic. However, it requires growing extensive amount of infectious virus that needs dedicated bio-safety facilities. In addition, it may be complicated to scale up the manufacturing for mass vaccination. In order to circumvent this, new approach that focuses more on scalable vaccine production, utilizes spike protein as the most promising antigen across the remaining platforms, such as protein subunit, and nucleic acid. Spike protein is present on the surface of the SARS-CoV-2, stimulates strong immune responses, and mediates entry into the host cells by binding to cell surface proteins ACE2 (Angiotensin-Converting Enzyme 2) receptors, that are essential for maintaining the viral life cycle.

Using whole-cell vaccine development approach, an Indian biopharmaceutical company, Bharat Biotech Private Limited, has developed "Covaxin" in collaboration with Indian Council of Medical Research (ICMR)-National Institute of Virology (NIV). The vaccine is derived using whole-virion inactivated Vero cell- derived platform technology. Inactivated vaccines do not replicate, and are therefore unlikely to revert, and cause pathological effects. They contain dead virus, incapable of infecting people, but, still able to instruct the immune system to mount an effective immune responses against a new infection. Covaxin has immune-enhancer, also known as vaccine adjuvant that is added to the vaccine to boost its immunogenicity. The advantage of using this vaccine is non-requirement of sub-zero storage facility, no reconstitution requirement, ready to use liquid presentation in multi-dose vials, and stable at 2-8°C. Importantly, Covaxin is equally effective against Variants of Concern (VOC) such as P.1- B.1.1.7 (Alpha), B.1.1.28 (Gamma), P.2-B.1.1.28 (Zeta), B.1.617.2 (Kappa), B.1.351 & B.1.617.2 (Beta & Delta).

Furthermore, two other biopharmaceutical companies, Sinovac and Sinopharm, have also made inactivated COVID-19 whole virus vaccines. Also, attenuated, whole-virus vaccines for COVID-19 were made by other biopharmaceutical companies as well. This type of vaccine contains the weakened SARS-CoV-2 virus, which is recognized by the immune system, without causing COVID-19 illness. This response builds immune memory that helps to fight off any SARS-CoV-2 infection in the future.

Lately, two Indian biopharmaceutical companies: the Serum Institute of India and Indian Immunologicals have developed COVID-19 vaccines using this approach. In addition, the vaccine developed by the Codagenix, using attenuated SARS- CoV-2, is currently under clinical trial.

Another vaccine development technology platform, the subunit protein vaccines use specific immunogenic pre-made protein from SARS-CoV-2 virus as antigen. Currently, many companies around the world are working to develop protein vaccines by targeting the spike protein of SARS-CoV-2. Major multinational companies such as Safoni/GSK are developing subunit vaccines in armyworms as expression host, while other companies are trying to express spike proteins in plant cells. Since in order to produce a robust immune response, the proteins need to be in active conformation to be fully functional, often, it is necessary to engineer proteins to stabilize the active conformation for immunization. The "molecular clamp" technology that is developed by the University of Queensland confers spike proteins to stay in active conformation prior to sticking it to the host cell.

Furthermore, interestingly, the Maryland-based company Novavax (USA) has developed a protein (subunit)-based SARS-CoV-2 vaccine called NVX-CoV2373. In March 2021, the company announced an efficacy rate of 96 per cent against the original SARS-CoV-2, 86 per cent against the B.11.7 variant, and 49 per cent against B.1.351 variant. To develop the vaccine, the researchers inserted a modified spike gene into another virus, called baculovirus, and allowed it to infect moth cell line (Sf9). The infected cells synthesize spike proteins and subsequently joined together to form spikes, as they do on the surface of the coronavirus. The researchers harvested the spike proteins from the cells, and assembled them into nanoparticles that mimicked the molecular structure of the SARS-CoV-2 virus, but, could not replicate or cause COVID-19 when introduced into the individuals as vaccine.

The vaccine consisting of many spike nanoparticles is primarily injected through an intra-mascular route with a compound extracted from the soapbark tree, that attracts immune cells to the site of injection, and causes them to respond more strongly to the nanoparticles. The APCs encounter the vaccine nanoparticles, allow them to get into the cells, tears apart the spike proteins, and subsequently display a portion of the fragments on its surface, that can be detected by helper T cells. The activated helper T cells, recruit other immune cells, including B-lymphocytes to respond to the vaccine antigen, and produce neutralizing antibodies against the spike proteins.

Nucleic acid vaccine technology platforms are also being used currently to develop effective vaccines against SARS-CoV-2 virus. In 1990, Fleger and colleagues published in "Science", their discovery that so-called "naked DNA" that is plasmid DNA that was previously been primarily used as transfecting agent, could also be directly injected into the muscle to express the encoded protein by the myocytes. The gene encoding the target protein is placed under the control of a mammalian promoter that regulates the expression of the gene in the plasmid vector construct.

There are several advantages of using plasmid DNA vaccine technology platform. First, the plasmid construct can be made rapidly in the laboratory. Second, adequate amplification by the immune system responding to any small amounts of the expressed protein encoded by the plasmid DNA, and third, intrinsic immunostimulatory properties of plasmid DNA make a compelling rationale for using this as vaccine technology platform. However, as of August 2016 no DNA vaccine had been approved in the US for human use. An Indian company Zydus Cadila has developed a COVID-19 vaccine using plasmid DNA platform technology, approved by DCGI (Drug Controller General of India) is the first DNA vaccine for human use. The company has applied to DCGI for EUA to launch ZyCoV-D, the world's first plasmid DNA vaccine for COVID-19. The plug and play technology on which the plasmid DNA platform is based is ideally suited for dealing with the emerging COVID-19 variants, as the plasmid construct can be easily adapted to produce effective immune responses against the highly transmissible COVID-19 variants.

Another type of nucleic acid vaccine technology platform uses viral vector; the most common is being the adenovirus. The advantage of using adenovirus is it causes mild cold, and asymptomatic infections in humans. The vaccine made by the University of Oxford in collaboration with AstraZeneca and Serum Institute of India, uses a chimpanzee adenovirus with the SARS-CoV-2 spike protein gene inserted into the genome. The reason behind using the chimpanzee virus is that humans do not have any pre-existing neutralizing antibodies to this adenovirus. It is possible that prior exposure to colds or infections may produce antibodies against the human adenovirus that might lower the efficacy of the vaccine by neutralizing the virus vector. The Russian Gamaleya Research Institute uses separate human adenovirus, so that vaccine efficacy can be improved, as in the case of chimpanzee adenovirus. The engineered adenovirus containing the spike gene of SARS-CoV-2 into its genome, enters the host cell by endocytosis, engulfed into a bubble, surrounded by lipid membrane, subsequently leaves the bubble, and injects its DNA into host cell nucleus, makes mRNA, and eventually releases the spike proteins to elicit a robust immune response against SARS-CoV-2.

Finally, the mRNA platform technology uses lipid-complexed mRNA encoding antigenic proteins. The mRNA vaccine inside the lipid-coated vesicle enters the cytosol after intramuscular administration of the vaccine. The ribosomes present in the cytosol translate the mRNA into spike proteins. The injected mRNA subsequently degrades. The spike proteins are secreted from the cell, and initiate an adaptive immune response. Using various activation pathways, immune cells elicit a cell-mediated and antibody-mediated protective immunity against the spike protein of SARS-CoV-2. The vaccines made by the major biopharmaceutical giant Pfizer (USA) and BioNTech (Germany), and by a startup biotech company Moderna (USA) in collaboration with the National Institute of Health (USA) have successfully developed mRNA vaccines against COVID-19 disease.

The future of vaccines

When COVID-19 became a worldwide pandemic, researchers were under immense pressure to develop a new vaccine in a very short timeframe. Due to unbelievable, fast-paced, technological improvements, new COVID-19 vaccines were made in record-breaking time.

Prior to the development of COVID-19 vaccines, the fastest development of a vaccine (Mumps) had been the four years approved back in the 1960s. The rapid pace of the generation of COVID-19 vaccines reveals a paradigm shift in vaccine development and deployment. It tells us how vaccines can be rapidly and effectively developed in short time frame against a new disease.

Historically, syringes have been vital for administrating vaccinations into individuals. However, the fear of inserting the needle and trypophobia are common in the population. A recent study indicates that about 20-50% of adolescents, and 20-30 % of young adults exhibit fear of needle insertions. Thus, it limits the mass vaccination, as many of the individuals will decline taking the vaccine due to phobia.

To overcome this issue, delivering vaccine through micro-patches has been developed. The method of patch-delivery has advantages as they are inexpensive to make and easy to store as opposed to syringe-delivered vaccines, that need to be stored at cold temperature to remain viable. Thus, patch-delivered vaccines are advantageous for vaccination in the rural, and poor communities, who fail to afford expensive vaccines.

Another remarkable development in vaccines manufacturing process is anti-idiotype antibodies. The idiotype (id) of an antibody molecule is the recognition site located at or near its antigen-binding site. Thus, the idiotype behaves as an antigenic site, when our body wants to make anti-antibody molecules, using a natural immune system mechanism, to control the levels of antibodies in the blood.

Furthermore, the antigen mimicry by anti-id antibodies produces surrogate antigen that can generate both humoral and cellular immune response. However, the greatest challenge of immunotherapy with the help of anti-id vaccines is to identify optimal anti-id antibody that will function as a true surrogate antigen. The advantages of anti-id vaccines over conventional vaccines are manifold: First, id-vaccines do not depend on the availability of large amounts of pure antigen, which is often a bottleneck factor in vaccine production; second, they can be easily coupled to potent immunogenic carriers, to become T cell-dependent antigen; third, it might be possible to produce fully synthetic id vaccines, using key sequence information from id hybridoma antigens; fourth, it is found that the specificities of vaccine-induced immune responses against tumors is higher for anti-id vaccines, as opposed to conventional antigen vaccines.

In addition, mRNA technology promises to revolutionize the development of future vaccines and treatment for cancer, and many other infectious diseases. Especially, for infectious disease, such as COVID-19, the new variants of the original strain of virus will continue to emerge in the future, that might escape immune protection in the body. Recent development of high-throughput next- generation sequencing (NGS) and genomic surveillance of the newly appeared variants will help us to design mRNA construct that codes for the mutant protein/antigen, based on sequence data of the variants, that take care of the mutations, causing a variant to evade immune protection.

However, while vaccines based on mRNA, such as those developed by Pfizer and Moderna, are highly effective and fast to develop, they are expensive to make, and must be stored at low temperatures. These factors pose challenges for LIMCs. Lately, researchers at Stanford University, USA, have created a prototype of a nanoparticle-based COVID-19 vaccine, that, they believe would not only be cheap, safe, and effective, but, also remain stable at room temperature. This vaccine is based on nanoparticles of an iron-containing protein, called ferritin. Each ferritin nanoparticle is studded with several of the spike proteins, that SARS-CoV-2 uses, to penetrate the host cells.

Finally, Avalon GloboCare, a leading US-based biotechnology company, has developed a mucosal intranasal spray vaccination against SARS-CoV-2. The company is using its S-layer technology, developed in collaboration with the Massachusetts Institute of Technology, USA, in an intranasal, spray vaccine candidate against SARS-CoV-2. The first-in-human clinical trials are planned in 2021. The S-layer nanoproteins are induced to assemble into spherical, ordered particles, that mimic the dimensions, and structure of the pathogenic virus. The vaccine candidate is essentially an artificial viral envelope that resembles the surface structure of SARS-CoV-2. These particles are themselves non-infectious. This candidate vaccine could provide first-line immune protection at the virus entrance site, and is complementary to any injectable vaccines, currently undergoing clinical trials.

Taken together, the effects of the recent COVID-19 pandemic on Indian society, and in other parts of the world have been devastating, and revival from it may take unusually longer period of time. For a diverse nation, such as India, in terms of geography, social behaviors, socio-economic condition, disparities in complying non-pharmaceutical interventions, across various states and/or union territories in the nation, along with disparities in individual state governance, it is sensible to assume, that, it would be advantageous to formulate one uniform hypothesis to combat the COVID-19 infection spread in the population, as opposed to using multiple hypotheses based on the multitude of parameters that might play roles in the COVID-19 disease transmission in India, and in other parts of the world. Thus, emphasize should be given for a uniform hypothesis, such as "Vaccine For All" to safeguard world population from getting infected, and further mitigate the severity of the disease, in COVID-19 victims. Recent technological advancement, such as genomic surveillance, using next generation sequencing (NGS), and efficient diagnostics, in the field of biotechnology, will help scientists to design vaccines quickly and effectively against any emerging strains/variants of COVID-19 in the future, including total eradication of these viral variants from the society. Moreover, the real-world vaccination data, as a result of massive nationwide vaccination drive, taken by the Government of India, and accessibility of data, in the public domain, are key to effectively monitor the performance of existing vaccines, against emerging variants, in the general population.

Figure 17. An overview of the different vaccine technology platforms against COVID-19. The stage of development for each of these platforms for COVID-19 vaccine development is indicated.

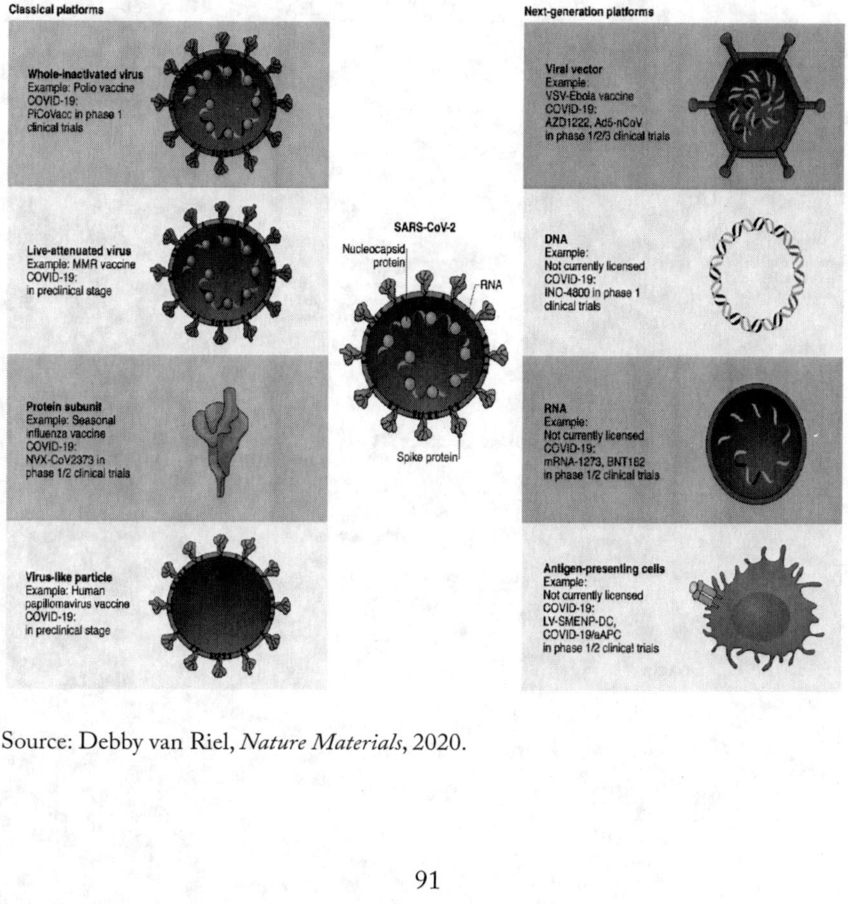

Source: Debby van Riel, *Nature Materials*, 2020.

Figure 18. An Overview of protein-based vaccine technology platform. Protein-based vaccine delivers disease-causing antigen, such as spike proteins directly into the human body, along with the adjuvant, priming the immune system to elicit a robust immune response against SARS-CoV-2 if it later infects the individuals.

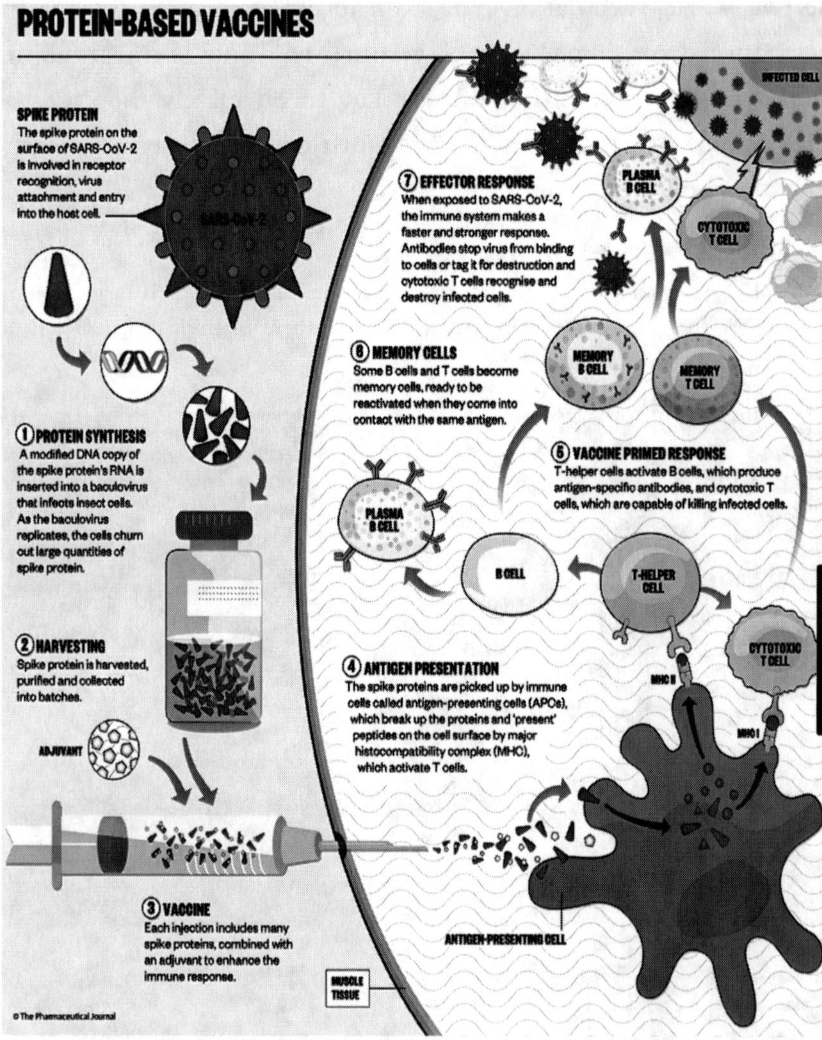

Source: The Pharmaceutical Journal.

Figure 19. An overview of adenoviral vector technology platform for vaccine development. Adenovirus vector vaccines use a common cold virus to deliver the genetic instructions for host cells to make SARS-CoV-2 spike protein, priming the immune system to attack the SARS-CoV-2 post-infection into individuals.

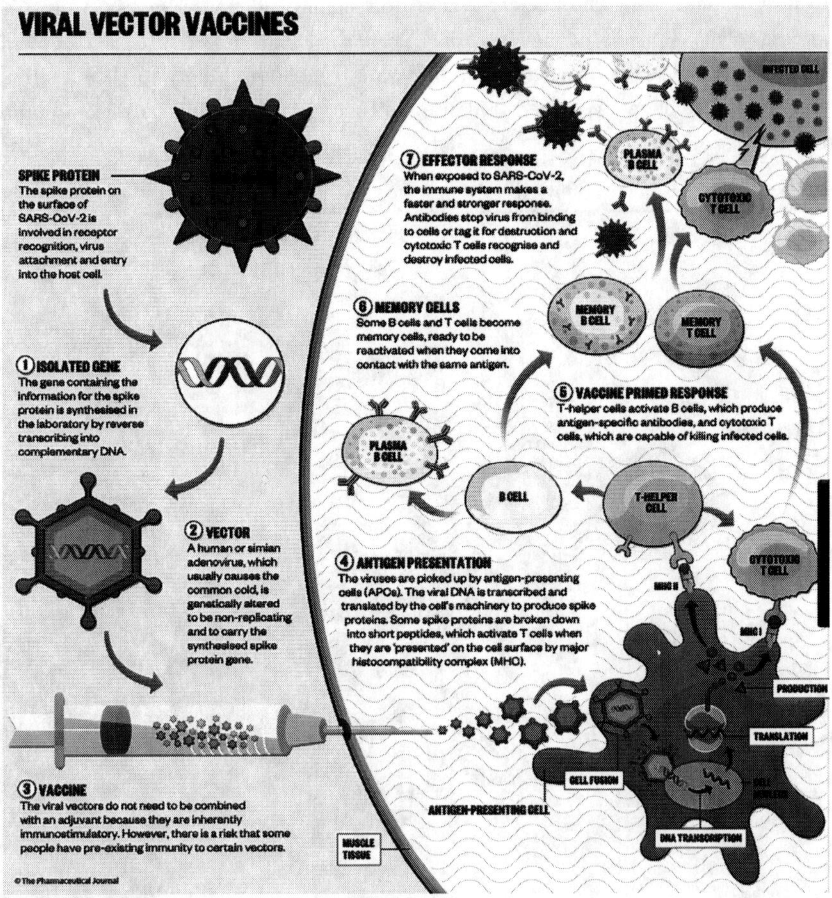

Source: The Pharmaceutical Journal.

Figure 20. An overview of DNA-based vaccine platforms. DNA vaccines consist of a synthetic DNA construct (plasmid) encoding the vaccine antigen. After uptake into the host cells, the vaccine antigen is expressed from the DNA construct under the direction of a promoter encoded in the genetic construct. The DNA constructs are translocated into host nucleus using the nuclear localization signal, and transcribed into protein-encoding mRNAs inside the nucleus. mRNAs are then translocated into the cytoplasm and form spike proteins using the host' protein synthesis machinery to elicit a strong antibody-mediated and cell-mediated immunity to protect individuals from future infections.

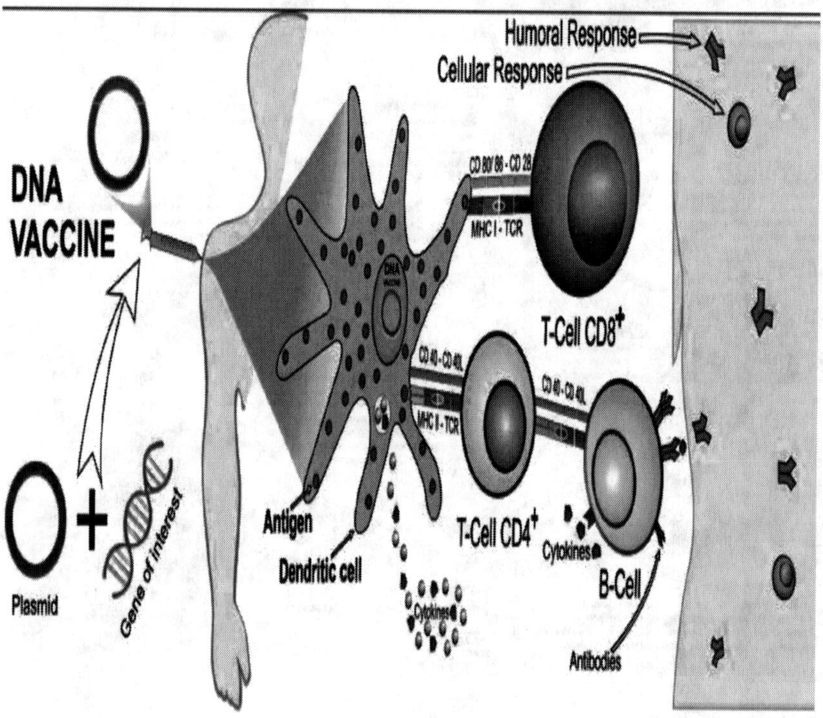

Source: Google Image

Figure 21. An overview of mRNA vaccine technology platform. mRNA vaccines introduce mRNA encoding a disease-specific antigen, such as spike proteins of SARS-CoV-2 and use host cells' protein synthesis machinery to produce antigens that elicit the immune response. The production of these foreign antigens within a vaccinated individual prepares the immune response to recognize, and fight off same infection more effectively. The cell-mediated immunity established by the vaccine lets cytotoxic T cells to kill the SARS-CoV-2-infected host cells. In addition, antibody (humoral)-mediated immunity, the spike antibodies made in the body neutralize the virus itself. mRNA vaccines mimic the natural virus' ability to trigger the body's immune response to new infection by both types of immunity.

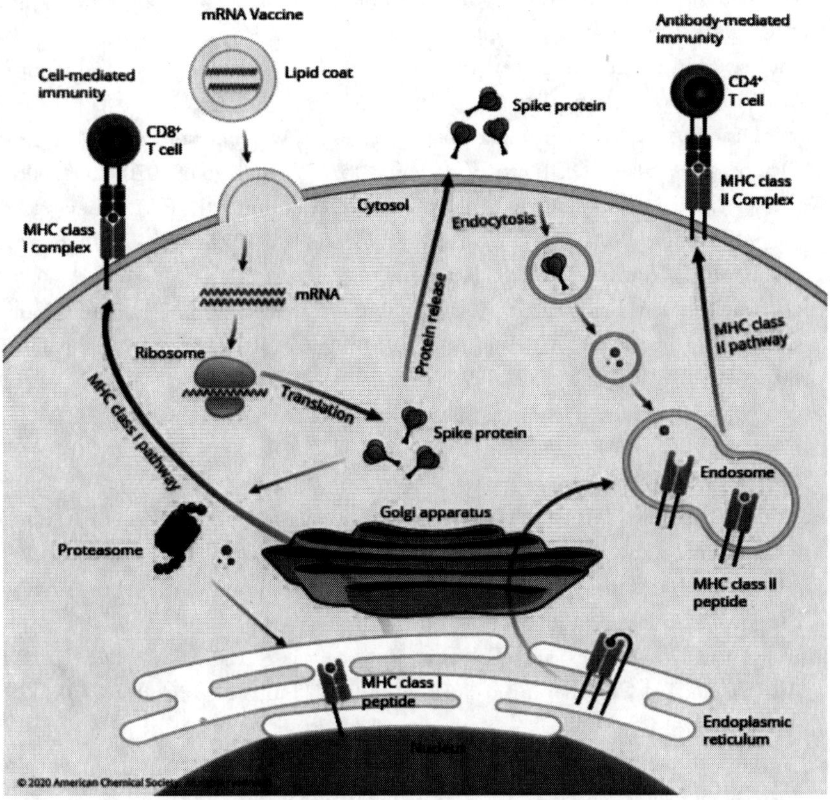

Source: American Chemical Society.

References

Vaccine Types. https://www.niaid.nih.gov/research/vaccine-types

Live-attenuated rabies virus co-infected with street rabies virus protects animals against rabies. X. Wu et al. *Vaccine.* 2011 June 6; 29(25): 4195-201. DOI: https://doi.org/10.1016/j.vaccine.2011.03.104.

Inactivated Viral Vaccines. B. Sanders, M. Koldijk, and H. Schuitemaker. Vaccine Analysis: Strategies, Principles, and Control. 2014 November 28: 45-80. DOI: https://doi.org/10.1007/978-3-662-45024-6_2

The Cutter Incident: How America's First Polio Vaccine Led to a Growing Vaccine Crisis. M. Fitzpatrick. *J R Soc Med.* 2006 March; 99(3): 156.

Vaccine failure explained. A. Mullard. *Nature* December 2008. DOI: https://doi.org/10.1038/news.2008.1302

Current Topics in Microbiology and Immunology. Measles. Pathogenesis and Control (2009). Editors: Griffin, Diane E, Oldstone, Michael B. A. (Eds).

Paralytic Disease Associated With Oral Polio Vaccines. D. A. Henderson et al. *JAMA.* 1964 October 5; 190:41-8. DOI: https://doi.org/10.1001/jama.1964.03070140047006.

Adverse event reports following yellow fever vaccination. N. P. Lindsey et al. *Vaccine.* Volume 26, Issue 48, November 11, 2008, P6077-6082. DOI: https://doi.org/10.1016/j.vaccine.2008.09.009

Association Between Pentavalent Rotavirus Vaccine and Severe Diarrhea Among Children in Nicaragua. M. Patel et al. *JAMA.* 2009; 301 (21): 2243-2251. DOI: https://doi.org/10.1001/jama.2009.756

Live attenuated vaccines: Historical successes and current challenges. P. D. Minor. *Virology.* Vol. 479-480, May 2015, P379-392. DOI: https://doi.org/10.1016/j.virol.2015.03.032

Zika Virus Vaccines. NIH-NIAID. https://www.niaid.nih.gov/diseases-conditions/zika-vaccines

Whooping Cough (Pertusis). Centers for Disease Control and Prevention. https://www.cdc.gov/vaccines/vpd/pertussis/index.html

Acellular Pertussis Vaccines and Pertussis Resurgence: Revise or Replace? C. M. Ausiello and A. Cassone. mBio 5(3): e01339-14. DOI: https://doi.org/10.1128/mBio.01339-14

The protective efficacy of polyvalent pneumococcal polysaccharide vaccine. E. D. Shapiro et al. *New England Journal of Medicine* 325 (21), 1453-1460, 1991.

A synthetic conjugate polysaccharide vaccine against Haemophilus influenza type b. V. Verez-Bencomo et al. *Science* 305 (5863), 522-525, 2004.

Glycoconjugate vaccines and immune interference: a review. R. Dagan et al. *Vaccine* 28 (34), 5513-5523, 2010.

Prevention of hepatitis B with the hepatitis B vaccine. G. A. Poland and R. M. Jacobson. *New England Journal of Medicine* 351 (27), 2832-2838, 2004.

A Vaccine Consisting of Recombinant *Borrelia burgdorferi* Outer-Surface Protein A to Prevent Lyme Disease. L. H. Sigal et al. *New England Journal of Medicine* 339 (4), 216-222, 1998.

The lyme disease vaccine: conception, development, and implementation. W. T. Thanassi and R. T. Schoen. *Annals of Internal Medicine* 132 (8), 661-668, 2000.

A review of vaccine research and development: meningococcal disease. M. P. Girard et al. *Vaccine* 24 (22), 4692-4700, 2006.

BEXSERO: Meningococcal Group B Vaccine. https://www.bexsero.com

Overview of Protein Expression. ThermoFisher SCIENTIFIC. https://www.thermofisher.com/in/en/home/life-science/protein-biology/protein-biology-learning-center/protein-biology-resource-library/pierce-protein-methods/overview-protein-expression-systems.html.

Multiple Post-translational Modifications Affect Heterogonous Protein Synthesis. A. A. Tokmakov et al. *J Biol Chem*. August 3; 287 (32): 27106-16. DOI: https://doi.org/10.1074/jbc.M112.366351.

GARDASIL. https://www.gardasil9.com

SHINGRIX. https://www.sningrix.com/index.html

Baculovirus as versatile vectors for protein expression in insects and mammalian cells. T. A. Kost et al. *Nature Biotechnology* 23, 567-575 (2005). DOI: https://doi.org/10.1038/nbt1095

Cervarix^{TM}: a vaccine for the prevention of HPV 16, 18-associated cervical cancer. A. Monie et al. *Biologics.* 2008 March 2(1): 107-113.

FluBlok, a next generation influenza vaccine manufactured in insect cells. *Biologicals.* 2009 Jun; 37(3): 182-9. DOI: https://doi.org/10.1016/j.biologicals.2009.02.014.

Virus Like Particles (VLP) as multivalent vaccine candidate against Chikungunya, Japanese Encephalitis, Yellow Fever and Zika Virus. H. Garg et al. *Scientific Reports* 10, Article Number: 4017 (2020). DOI: https://doi.org/10.1038/s41598-020-61103-1.

Self-assembling protein nanoparticles in the design of vaccines. J. Lopez-Sagaseta et al. *Computational and Structural Biotechnology* Journal Volume 14, 2016. P58-68. DOI: https://doi.org/10.1016/j.csbj.2015.11.001.

Recent Advances in Subunit Vaccine Carriers. A. Vartak and S. J. Sucheck. *Vaccines* 2016, 4(2), 12. DOI: https://doi.org/10.3390/vaccines4020012.

Nano-carriers of COVID-19 vaccines: main pillars of efficacy. C. Constantin et al. *Future Medicine* October 11, 2021. DOI: https://doi.org/10.2217/nnm-2021-0250.

Genetic Immunization Is a Simple Method for Eliciting an Immune Response. D.C. Tang et al. *Nature,* 356, 1992, 152-154. DOI: http://dx.doi.org/10.1038/356152a0

The promise of nucleic acid vaccines. N. P. Restifo et al. *Gene Ther.* 2000 Jan; 7(2): 89-92. DOI: https://doi.org/10.1038/sj.gt.3301117.

Developments in Viral Vector-Based Vaccines. T. Ura et al. *Vaccines* (Basel). 2014 Sep; 2(3): 624-641. DOI: https://doi.org/10.3390/vaccines2030624.

Viral Vectors for COVID-19 Vaccine Development. K. Lundstrom. *Viruses.* 2021 Feb 19; 13(2): 317. DOI: https://doi.org/10.3390/v13020317.

Adneoviral vector vaccine platforms in the SARS-CoV-2 pandemic. S. A. Mendonca et al. *npj Vaccines* 6, 97 (2021). DOI: https://doi.org/10.1038/s41541-021-00356-x

The tangled history of mRNA vaccines. E. Dolgin. 2021. https://www.nature.com/articles/d41586-021-02483-w

mRNA vaccines-a new era in vaccinology. N. Pardi et al. *Nat Rev Drug Discov* 17, 261-279 (2018). DOI: https://doi.org/10.1038/nrd.2017.243.

In Gratitude for mRNA Vaccines. L. M. Stuart. *N Engl J Med* 2021; 385:1436-1438. DOI: https://doi.org/10.1056/NEJMcibr2111445.

Efficacy and Safety of the mRNA-1273 SARS-CoV-2 Vaccine. L.R. Baden et al. *N Engl J Med* 2021; 384:403-416. DOI: https://doi.org/10.1056/NEJMoa2035389.

Safety and Efficacy of the BNT162b2 mRNA Covid-19 Vaccine. F.P. Polack et al. *N Engl J Med* 2020; 383:2603-2615. DOI: https://doi.org/10.1056/NEJMoa2034577.

Meet the mRNA vaccine rookies aiming to take down COVID-19. https://www.cas.org/resource/blog/covidmrna-vaccine.

A COVID-19 Vaccine: Big Strides Come with Big Challenges. J. Mellet and M.S. Pepper. *Vaccines* 2021, 9(1), 39. DOI: https://doi.org/10.3390/vaccines9010039.

A Comprehensive Review of the Global Efforts on COVID-19 Vaccine Development. Y. Li et al. *ACS Cent. Sci.* 2021, 7,4, 512-533. DOI: https://doi.org/10.1021/acscentsci.1c00120.

An overview of current COVID-19 vaccine platforms. A. Nagy et al. Computational and Structural Biotechnology Journal. Volume 19, 2021, P2508-2517. DOI: https://doi.org/10.1016/j.csbj.2021.04.061.

Everything you need to know about COVID-19 vaccines. https://pharmaceuticaljournal.com/article/feature/everything-you-need-to-know-about-covid19-vaccines.

Tech Factsheets for Policymakers: Fall 2020 Series. Vaccine Platforms. T. Cushing & A. Jayanti. HARVARD Kennedy School. BELFER CENTER for Science and International Affairs.

Developing Covid-19 Vaccines at Pandemic Speed. N. Lourie et al. *N Engl J Med.* 2020 May 21; 382(21): 1969-1973. DOI: https://doi.org/10.1056/NEJMp2005630.

SARS-CoV-2 Vaccines: Status Report. F. Amanat et al. *Immunity.* 2020 Apr 14; 52(4): 583-589. DOI: https://doi.org/10.1016/j.immuni.2020.03.007.

India's New COVID-19 DNA Vaccine for Adolescents and Adults Is a First. J. Abbasi. *JAMA.* 2021; 326(14): 1365. DOI: https://doi.org/10.1001/jama.2021.16625.

DBT-BIRAC supported ZyCoV-D developed by Zydus Cadila Receives Emergency Use Authorization. https://pib.gov.in/PressReleasePage.aspx?PRID=1747669.

DNA vaccine candidate encoding SARS-CoV-2 spike proteins elicited potent humoral and Th1 cell-mediated immune responses in mice. E. Prompetchara et al. *PLoS ONE* 16(3): e0248007. DOI: https://doi.org/10.1371/journal.pone.0248007.

Extended delivery of vaccines to the skin improves immune responses. J. C. Joyce et al. *Journal of Controlled Release*. Vol. 304, 28 Jun 2019, P135-145. DOI: https://doi.org/10.1016/j.jconrel.2019.05.006.

The anti-idiotypic vaccines for immunotherapy. M. Bhattacharya-Chatterjee et al. *Curr Opin Mol Ther.* 2001 February; 3(1): 63-9.

The promise of Anti-idiotype Revisited. H. Kohler et al. *Front. Immunol.* 12 April 2019. DOI: https://doi.org/10.3389/fimmu.2019.00808.

S-layer fusion proteins-construction principles and applications. N. IIK et al. *Curr Opin Biotecnol.* 2011 December; 22(6): 824-831. DOI: https://doi.org/10.1016/j.copbio.2011.05.510.

Real-World Effectiveness of Vaccines: Evolution of COVID-19 Variants and Their Immune Escape Mechanisms

> "We've ascribed far too much human authority over the [COVID-19] virus."
>
> – New York Times

> "….there can be no more illusions of inevitability. The flu, it turns out, has always been a choice. Now we have the opportunity to do something about it-and the burden of knowing we can."
>
> –Anonymous

> "The [COVID] Delta variant is clearly going to be another wave. If you decide not to get vaccinated, this virus will still find you."
>
> – CBS News, Jun 25, 2021

Real-world effectiveness of vaccines

Vaccine effectiveness is primarily measured by analyzing real-world evidence. Clinical trials on a cohort of volunteers provide a good indication about how well the vaccine works, and its safety profile. In contrast, real-world evidence helps people better understand if a vaccine is effective in day-to-day clinical practice, as opposed to "Vaccine Efficacy" (VE), that is determined in controlled clinical trials. Thus, in combination with clinical trial-derived vaccine efficacy data, real-world evidence, gives us the bigger picture about how effective a vaccine in larger, more heterogeneous population with different ethnicities, and in various healthcare settings, across the world over an extended period of time. By using these evidences, scientists, clinicians, regulators, and governments can effectively monitor the contribution of a vaccine to the society.

The real-world effectiveness of a vaccine is 3-fold: (a) it helps government, healthcare providers, and communities to precisely understand how well a specific vaccine is working across demographics; (b) developing key supporting strategies, to increase vaccine uptake in the society, to protect lives, and reduce hospitalizations; (c) informing longer-term use of a vaccine, and necessary adjustments to be made, that might give additional protection to individuals, in terms of vaccine boosters, dosing or combination treatment.

There are several ways to determine how well a vaccine works to protect individuals from an infectious disease. As the number of people vaccinated against COVID-19 grows, important real-world vaccination data emerge, which is helping to understand the vaccine effectiveness. First, we are beginning to understand, whether a vaccine is reducing deaths, and case fatalities in hospitalized patients to milder form of COVID-19 disease. Second, whether it is reducing the rates of new infections, across the population. Third, if it is preventing the transmission, and speed of the SARS-CoV-2 virus in infecting individuals. Fourth, whether it is effective against all ages, race, ethnicity, and those who have underlying co-morbidities such as asthma, cancer, diabetes, cardiovascular diseases, and HIV.

Furthermore, most of the COVID-19 vaccines work, by priming the body's natural immunity, so that it can act quickly, and effectively if someone encounters the virus as a result of breakthrough infection. Thus, using the real-world vaccination data, it is possible to better understand the effectiveness of a vaccine. Also, as vaccination programs continue around the world, the comprehensive results of the immunogenicity studies of a vaccine will help us to determine the nature of immune response, that a vaccine triggers, and how long it lasts. Additionally, data will help inform the right dose of a vaccine, as well as, if and when booster vaccinations may be required.

In addition, logistical aspects, and ease of use are critical, to ensure broad access to, and uptake of a vaccine. This includes, how easily a vaccine can be transported using a cold chain that is primarily used for other licensed vaccines. Stability and duration of the stability of a vaccine are also key considerations that can be addressed, using real-world vaccination data. Also, how easily it can be administered within existing healthcare settings, and need for any specially trained medical staffers is needed, are also addressed.

Thus, evidence of real-world effectiveness, together with data from clinical trial is improving our knowledge, if a vaccine is working, as anticipated, based on initial clinical trial results. Importantly, as new variants of the original virus strain develop, as the pandemic progresses, the initial vaccination data on individuals infected with the previous strain of virus that appeared in the initial phase of the pandemic, may no longer valid, unless, we determine, whether a vaccine is protecting individuals, against the new variants. Thus a long duration of real-world vaccination data, in course of the pandemic, will better figure out the effectiveness of a vaccine, in combating the infectious disease, in majority of the population.

History of evolution of COVID-19 variants, and immune escape mechanisms

SARS-CoV-2 (COVID-19) is the seventh member in the human coronavirus group that infects human respiratory organs. The other six are: Coronavirus- 229E (HCoV-229E) which appeared in 1965, Coronavirus-OC43 (HCoV-OC43) in 1967, Severe Acute Respiratory Syndrome Coronavirus (SARS-CoV) in 2002, Coronavirus NL63

(HCOV-NL-63) in 2004, Coronavirus HKU1 (HKU1) in 2005, and Middle East Respiratory Syndrome Coronavirus (MERS-CoV) in 2012.

Moreover, the nucleotide sequence of SARS-CoV-2 shows 79.9 per cent similarity with that of SARS-CoV sequence. However, when amino acid sequence of three different proteins, such as envelope protein E, nucleocapsid protein N, and spike protein of S of SARS-CoV and SARS-CoV-2 were compared, they show 96 per cent, 89.6 per cent, and 77 per cent similarity respectively. This shows that, variation is more in the spike protein sequence, as opposed to two other proteins, E and S, between two strains of coronaviruses. Thus, presumably, the S protein is more vulnerable to mutational changes compared to E and N proteins, giving rise to new strains of coronoviruses and/or new variant(s) of an existing coronavirus strain, such as SARS-CoV-2. Indeed, till date, all of the SARS-CoV-2 variants, that appeared during the ongoing COVID-19 pandemic, have mutations in the spike protein, more specifically, in the receptor binding domain (RBD), of the spike protein of the virus, resulting variation in the transmissibility, infectivity, susceptibility toward existing COVID-19 vaccines, and synthetically produced monoclonal antibodies, targeted against receptor binding protein, of the spike protein.

As of April 2012, SARS-CoV-2 virus, that causes COVID-19 disease, accounted for more than 143 million infections, and more than three million deaths worldwide. With the rapid emergence of COVID-19 mutants, virus genomic sequences are being generated, and shared across the world, at an unprecedented rate. There are more than one million SARS-CoV-2 sequences, available via the Global Initiative of Sharing All Influenza Data (GISAID), that allows near real-time surveillance, of the unfolding, of the ongoing COVID-19 pandemic. This high throughput genomic sequencing of SARS-

CoV-2, enables scientists, to identify the emerging variants, and sets of mutations, potentially causing changes, in the viral properties, in terms of transmissibility, in the population, and the severity of the COVID-19 disease, allows near real-time surveillance, of the unfolding, of the ongoing COVID-19 pandemic.

However, the high-effect mutations in the SARS-CoV-2 genome, that contribute to virus adaptation, and fitness, tend to occur in the minority population, as opposed to well tolerated, low-effect or no-effect 'neutral' amino acid changes. The fitness-enhancing mutations, that change virus properties, in terms of pathogenicity, infectivity, transmissibility and/or antigenicity, were first detected, within a few months, of the evolution of SARS-CoV-2 in humans. For example, the amino acid change in the spike protein (D614G), was first observed in April 2020, and emerged multiple times, in the global SARS-CoV- 2 population. Interestingly, its coding sequence exhibits a high dN/dS ratio (>1 positive selection, <1 negative selection, and =1 neutral selection), indicating positive selection, at the codon position 614. However, subsequent studies indicated that D614G confers a moderate advantage for infectivity. The key is to identify mutations that affect the antigenic phenotype of SARS-CoV-2 that will enable variants, to overcome immunity, conferred by natural infection or through vaccination.

There is increasing evidence that mutations that changes the antigenic phenotype of SARS-CoV-2, are arising at an alarming pace that requires immediate attention. Tracking of the evolution of SARS-CoV-2, from December 2019 to October 2020, has revealed, virus, acquiring about two mutations, per month, in the global population, following the emergence of D614G and N439K in Scotland, in March 2020. With the quick disappearance of first lineage of N439K (B.1.141), another lineage, that independently acquired N439K (B.1.1.298), emerged, and circulated widely, in many European countries. N439K variant and its lineages, enhance the binding affinity of RBD of spike protein of SARS-CoV-2, for the ACE2 receptor, and reduce the neutralizing activity, of some monoclonal antibodies, and polyclonal antibodies, isolated from sera, in people, who have recovered from COVID-19 disease. Moreover, another RBD amino acid change, Y43F, has been shown to be associated with increased ACE2-binding affinity; the first lineage was identified in Denmark (B.1.1.298). The B.1.1.298 lineage also has Δ69-70, an amino-terminal domain (NTD) deletion, including in the second N439K lineage, B.1.258. Δ69-70, which is likely, to alter the conformation of an exposed NTD (N-Terminal Domain) loop, and, is shown to be associated, with increased infectivity, of SARS-CoV-2. Also, genomic analyses indicate a change, in the host environment, and various types of increased selective pressures, regulate immunologically dominant SARS-CoV-2 genes, resulting emergence of variants, with larger numbers of mutation, compared to previous circulating variants. These lineages were named 'variants of concern', due to their enhanced transmission abilities, in the humans.

A detailed immunogenicity studies of these variants, in terms of their ability to escape immune mechanisms, in the host, by examining the level of cross- protection, provided by the earlier viruses, that were first emerged, in the beginning of the ongoing COVID-19 pandemic, and which were used, in all of the current vaccine preparations, will be helpful in combating the further spread of transmission, due to these variants, by designing reformulated vaccines, from the previous versions. Many of the ongoing structural studies, key mutations identified in viruses, using monoclonal or polyclonal antibody-mediated viral neutralization assays, targeted investigation of mutations, by site-directed mutagenesis, and deep mutational scanning (DMS) experiments, that identify the possibility of further mutations in the variants, will shed light on the detailed antigenic profile of the spike mutations, and their roles, in the immune escape mechanisms, within the host cells.

Serological analyses of about 650 individuals, infected with SARS-CoV-2, indicated that approximately 90 per cent of neutralizing activity of the antibodies, found in plasma or serum, target spike protein's RBD. Furthermore, structural analyses, using antibody footprints, allowed the categorization of RBD-binding neutralizing antibodies, into four classes: ACE2- blocking antibodies, that bind the spike protein in the open conformation (class 1), and both open and closed conformation (class 2); antibodies, that fail to block ACE2, and bind the RBD, in both the open conformation, and the closed conformation (class 3); and neutralizing antibodies, that bind outside of ACE2 site, and only, in the open conformation (class 4).

Although, the RBD is immunodominant, evidence, tends to suggest, that the N-terminal domain (NTD) of the spike protein is immunogenic, as well. However, the mechanism of neutralization mediated by the NTD-specific antibodies, remains to be fully elucidated. Interestingly, an NIH-funded study, published recently in *Science*, revealed the granular picture of the array of antibodies, till date, against SARS-CoV-2, found in people, who have recovered from mild cases of COVID-19. It was observed that vast majority of the antibodies (about 84 per cent) were targeted other portion of the spike proteins, thān the RBD. This strongly suggests, that an effective immune response does not necessarily targeted, against the RBD only. It encompasses antibodies, directed against areas, across the entire spike protein. Furthermore, the researchers were able to show that NTD-directed antibodies do indeed neutralize SARS-CoV-2, in the culture. NTD mutates frequently, especially, in several emerging variants of concern. In addition, about 40 per cent of the circulating antibodies, target another portion of the spike, called the S2 subunit. Thus, S2 subunit might be a potential target, for a possible pan-coronavirus vaccine, since this portion of the spike, is highly conserved in SARS-CoV-2, and related coronaviruses. Also, a recent study, published in *Science*, shows that SARS-CoV-2 often mutates, by deleting small pieces of its genetic code. Although, the virus has its own "proofreading" mechanism, that fixes errors as virus replicates, a deletion won't show up on the proofreader's radar. These deletions frequently occur in similar spots on the genome. These are sites, where antibodies would bind to, and neutralize the virus. But, due to these deletions, certain antibodies, fail to recognize the virus.

SARS-CoV-2 has the capacity to evade immunity by bypassing the innate immune system. For example, the COVID-19 variant, B.1.1.7 has a sub-genomic RNA message, that instructs a protein (ORF9b) to be made, that regulates innate immune system's response, to virus, by inhibiting interferon-1 production, that prevents viral replication. Indeed, antibodies against ORF9b were present in the sera of convalescent coronovirus patients. Moreover, the lymphocyte count is found to be associated, with increased disease severity in COVID-19 patients. Lymphopenia, and lower lymphocyte counts, indicate a poor prognosis of the COVID-19 disease. It is possible that SARS-CoV-2 might have direct effect on T cells, potentially through apoptosis, and evades host's immune system. Besides, lymphocytes, other innate immune cells, such as neutrophils and neutrophil-associated cytokines, CXCL2 and CXCL8, are found to be elevated, in the blood and serum of COVID- 19 patients. Natural killer (NK) cells, cytotoxic T lymphocytes (C8+), macrophages, and dendritic cells (DC) are key component of innate/cellular immunity. Their numbers and functions are reduced in COVID-19 patients. Dysregulation of macrophage activation syndrome is observed in patients, infected with COVID-19. Thus, it is possible that restoration of impaired functions, of four key components of innate immune system, can possibly prevent the virus, to escape immune mechanisms, in the COVID-19 infected patients.

Taken together, there is substantial evidence, in the scientific literatures, about the changing antigenicity, of the SARS-CoV-2 spike protein, in the variants, that affect antibody neutralization. The amino acid substitutions, and deletions in the spike protein of the virus, that negate the neutralizing activities of the antibodies, are happening, in increasing frequencies, in various emerging variants, of COVID-19. Thus, a thorough understanding of the consequences of spike mutations, for antigenicity, along with mechanisms of impairment, in cell-mediated innate immunity, among variants, will help scientists to develop more effective interventional strategy, against COVID-19 disease.

Thus, an in-depth follow-up study, on the progression of mass vaccination, and its effect, on the COVID-19 caseloads, and severity of the disease, in the entire world, as we go through the successive waves of the ongoing COVID-19 pandemic, will further validate, the real-world effectiveness of the existing, and newly developed COVID-19 vaccines, against new COVID-19 variants.

Figure 22. The list of SARS-CoV-2 variants that includes worrisome, concerning, and investigational viruses.

Alpha B.1.1.7	It was first identified in UK in September 2020 and since then has circulated into 173 countries. It was observed that female patients more likely to require intensive care and die from it. It is classified under 'variants of concern'.
Beta B.1.351	It was first discovered in South Africa in August 2020 and since then has transmitted into 122 countries around the world. It is classified under 'variants of concern'.
Gamma P.1	It was initially found in Manaus. Brazil in December 2020 and has circulated into 74 countries. It is classified under 'variants of concern'.
Delta B.1.617.2	This highly infectious virus was originated in India. It has a mutated sub-variant Delta Plus that is infectious as well. Delta version is 55.5 percent more transmissible than Alpha variety. It is classified under 'variants of concern'.
Eta	It was first detected in UK followed by in Nigeria. It needs further attention. It is classified under 'variant of interest'.
lota	There was a surge of lota cases initially in New York City. However, more transmissible Alpha has now overtaken it. It is is classified under 'variants of interest'.
Kappa	It is the sub-lineage of B.1.617 (Delta). Two cases were first reported in India. It is classified under 'variant of interest'.
Lambda	It was first detected in Peru in December 2020. Accounting for 80 per cent of the cases in the country. It has circulated into 29 other countries excluding India. It is classified under 'variants of interest'.
Epsilon	It was first found in California, USA. It is classified under 'alerts for further monitoring'.
Zeta	It was first observed in Rio de Janeiro, Brazil. It is classified under 'alerts for further monitoring'.
Theta	It was first observed simultaneously in Philippines and Japan. It is classified under 'alerts for further monitoring'.

Source: Adapted from Times of India.

Figure 23. Viral cartography: the antigenic map of different COVID-19 variants, indicating the distance between a new variant and original Wuhan strain, and the distance between the two variants indicates how well antibodies against one variant neutralize the other.

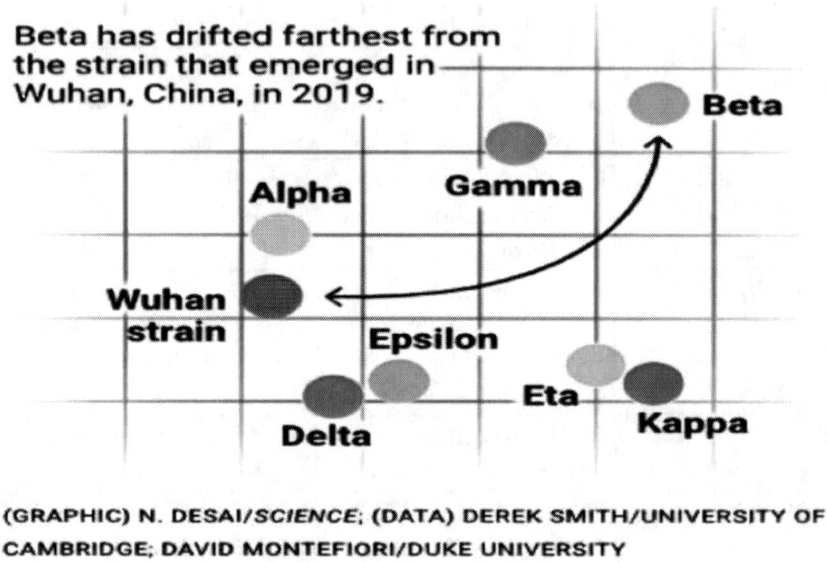

Source: University of Cambridge and Duke University.

Figure 24. The domain organization of the SARS-CoV-2 spike protein indicating amino acid sequence variability. The spike protein is synthesized as 1,273 amino acid polypeptide, and the frequency of amino acid variants, including both for substitutions and deletions, at each of the positions is shown. These variants, relative to the Wuhan-Hu-1 reference sequence, were identified with the use of CoV-GLUE that filters out Global Initiative on Sharing All Influenza Data (GISAID) sequences identified as being low quality or from non-human hosts (sequences retrieved from the GISAID database on 3 February 2021). Among 426,623 genomes after filtering, 5,106 different amino acid replacements or substitutions across 1,267 spike proteins were identified. Among which 320 at 259 positions were observed in at least 100 sequences. Several deletions were also identified especially with the amino-terminal domain (NTD). The most frequently found NTD deletions are the two-residue deletion at position 69 and 70 (Δ 69-70), present in 45,898 sequences. The S1-S2 boundary is at amino acid position 685.

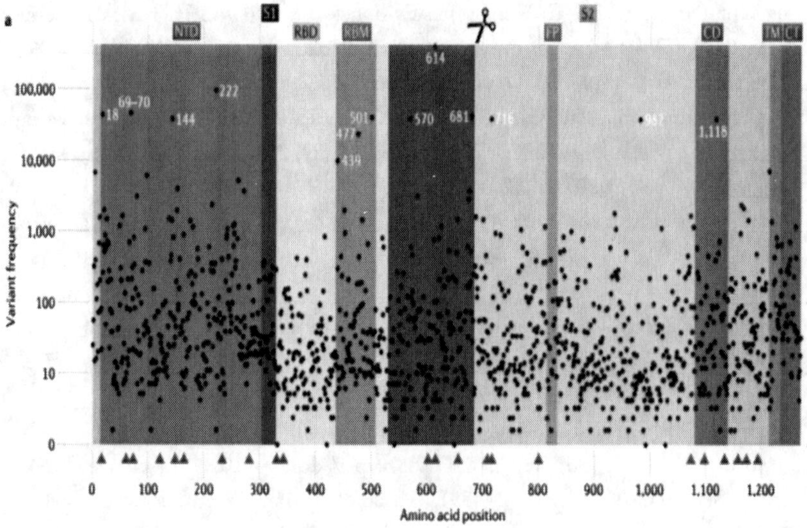

Source: W.T. Harvey et al. *Nat Rev Microbiol* 2021.

References

World Health organization (W.H.O). Statement on the benefits of vaccines against COVID-19.

Real world effectiveness of covid-19 vaccines. D. Hungerford et al. *BMJ* 2021; 374. DOI: https://doi.org/10.1136/bmj.n2034.

How CDC Monitors COVID-19 Vaccine Effectiveness. https://www.cdc.gov/coronavirus/2019-ncov/vaccines/effectiveness/how-they-work.htlm.

AstraZeneca: Real-World Evidence and Vaccine Effectiveness Explained. 18 June 2021. https://www.astrazeneca.com/what-science-can-do/topics/covid-19/real-world-evidence-and-vaccine-effectiveness-explained.html.

Coronavirus-2019: Origin and evolution. N. C. Mandal. *Journal of Hematology and Allied Sciences.* Vol. 1. Issue 1. January-April 2021. DOI: https://doi.org/10.25259/JHAS_8_2021).

W.H.O Coronavirus (COVID-19) Dashboard. https://covid19.who.int.

Rapid implementation of SARS-CoV-2 sequencing to investigate cases of health-care associated COVID-19: a prospective genomic surveillance study. Meredith LW et al. *THE LANCET Infectious Disease.* Volume 20, Issue 11, P1263-1271, 2020. DOI: https://doi.org/10.1016/S1473-3099(20)30562-4.

Neutral Theory and Rapidly Evolving Viral Pathogens. S.D.W. Frost et al. *Mol Biol Evol.* 2018 Jun 1; 35(6): 1348-1354. DOI: https://doi.org/10.1093/molbev/msy088.

Tracking Changes in SARS-CoV-2 Spike: Evidence that D614G Increases Infectivity of the COVID-19 Virus. B. Korber et al. *Cell* 2020 Aug 20; 182(4): 812-827.e19. DOI: https://doi.org/10.1016/j.cell.2020.06.043.

Structural and Functional Analysis of the D614G SARS-CoV-2 Spike Protein Variant. L.Yurkovetskiy et al. *Cell.* 2020 October 29; 183(3): 739-758.e8. DOI: https://doi.org/10.1016/j.cell 2020.09.032.

SARS-CoV-2 variants, spike mutations and immune escape. W.T. Harvey et al. *Nature Review Microbiology* 19, 409-424 (2021). DOI: https://doi.org/10.1038/s41579-021-00573-0.

Evaluating The Effects of SARS-CoV-2 Spike Mutations D614G on Transmissibility and Pathogenicity. E. Volz et al. *Cell* Vol. 184, Issue 1, 7 January 2021, P64-75.e11. DOI: https://doi.org/10.1016/j.cell.2020.11.020.

The Emergence of SARS-CoV-2 in Europe and North America. M. Worobey et al. *Science* Oct 30; 370(6516): 564-570. DOI: https://doi.org/10.1126/science.abc8169.

Circulating SARS-CoV-2 spike N439K variants maintain fitness while evading antibody-mediated immunity. E. C. Thomson et al. *Cell* Vol. 184, Issue 5, 4 March 2021, P1171-1187.e20. DOI: https://doi.org/10.1016/j.cell.2021.01.037.

J. Fonager et al. https://files.ssi.dk/Mink-cluster-5-short- report_AFO2 (2020).

Recurrent emergence and transmission of SARS-CoV-2 Spike deletion H69/V70 and its role in the Alpha variant B.1.1.7. B. Meng et al. *Cell Reports.* 35, 109292 June 29, 2021. DOI: https://doi.org/10.1016/j.celrep.2021.109292.

Mapping Neutralizing and Immunodominant Sites on the SARS-CoV-2 Spike Receptor-Binding Domain By Structure-Guided High-Resolution Serology. L. Piccoli et al. *Cell* 2020 November 12; 183(4): 1024-1042.e21. DOI: https://doi.org/10.1016/j.cell.2020.09.037.

SARS-CoV-2 neutralizing antibody structures inform therapeutic strategies. C.O. Barnes et al. *Nature* 588, 682-687 (2020). DOI: https://doi.org/10.1038/s41586-020-2852-1.

Aerodynamic analysis of SARS-CoV-2 in two Wuhan hospitals. Y. Liu et al. *Nature* 582, 557-560 (2020). DOI: https://doi.org/10.1038/s41586-020-2271-3.

N-terminal domain antigenic mapping reveals a site of vulnerability for SARS-CoV-2. M. McCallum et al. *Cell* 2021 April 29; 184(9): 2332-2347.e16. DOI: https://doi.org/10.1016/j.cell.2021.03.028.

Neutralizing and protective human monoclonal antibodies recognizing the N-terminal domain of the SARS-CoV-2 spike protein. N. Suryadevara et al. *Cell* 2021 Apr 29; 184(9): 2316-2331.e15. DOI: https://doi.org/10.1016/j.cell.2021.03.029.

Prevalent, protective, and convergent IgG recognition of SARS-CoV-2 non-RBD spike epitopes. W. N. Voss et al. *Science.* 2021 June 4; 372(6546): 1108-1112. DOI: https://doi.org/10.1126/science.abg5268.

Recurrent deletions in the SARS-CoV-2 spike glycoprotein drive antibody escape. K.R. MaCarthy et al. *Science*. 2021 March 12; 371(6534): 1139-1142. DOI: https://doi.org/10.1126/science.abf6950.

SARS corona virus peptides recognized by antibodies in the sera of convalescent cases. J. Guo. *Virology* Vol. 324, Issue 2, 1 July 2004, P 251-256. DOI: https://doi.org/10.1016/j.virol.2004.04.017.

Clinical predictors of mortality due to COVID-19 based on an analysis of data of 150 patients from Wuhan, China. Q. Ruan et al. *Intensive Care Med.* 2020. May; 46(5): 846-848. DOI: https://doi.org/10.1007/s00134-020-05991-x.

Innate immune response of human alveolar type II cells infected with severe acute respiratory syndrome-coronavirus. Z. Qian et al. *Am J Respir Cell Mol Biol.* 2013 Jun; 48(6): 742-8. DOI: https://doi.org/10.1165/rcmb.2012-03390C.

Monocyte and dendritic cell defects in COVID-19. A. Wack. *Nature Cell Biology* 23, 445-447 (2021). DOI: https://doi.org/10.1038/s41556-021-00685-y.

Complex Immune Dysregulation in COVID-10 Patients with Severe Respiratory Failure. J. Evangelos J et al. *Cell Host & Microbe* 2020 June 10; 27(6): 992-1000.e3. DOI: https://doi.org/10.1016/j.chom.2020.04.009.

The Benefits of Vaccination: Health, Economic, and Social Perspectives

"We need the serenity to accept the things we cannot change, courage to change the things we can, and the wisdom to know the difference."

– Lucy McBride

"Bottom line, is that we've got to get the entire world vaccinated, not just our own country, otherwise every year there will be another threat as more mutants come by."

– Anthony Fauci

"We're going to see [COVID-19] hills and valleys, at least for the next several years as we get more vaccine out. That's going to help.... But I can just tell you, this is a coronavirus forest fire that will not stop until it finds all the human wood that it can burn."

– Bloomberg, Sep 12, 2021

The development of safe and efficacious vaccination, against diseases that result substantial morbidity, and mortality has been one of the fascinating scientific advances of the 21st century. Other than safe water, no other modality has had such an enormous effect in reducing the mortality rates, and population growth. It is estimated that vaccines have prevented 6 million deaths from diseases annually.

By 2055, the world's population is estimated to reach about 10 billion, that is, in part, due to effective vaccination programs, worldwide, preventing diseases, and prolonging life expectancy, along with quality-adjusted-life-years (QALYs) in the population. Agencies, such as W.H.O, United Nations Children's Fund (UNICEF), Gavi, the Vaccine Alliance, The Coalition for Epidemic Preparedness Initiative (CEPI), and The Bill & Melinda Gates Foundation have been instrumental in expanding vaccine coverage across the world.

As clinicians and biomedical scientists, primarily concentrate on the health benefits, that vaccine provide, it is important to discuss, the economic and social benefits apart from health, that have been impacted human lives, across all regions, and all age groups, to better understand a comprehensive benefits of vaccines, in the society. Moreover, it is equally important to effectively communicate, the social and economic benefits of vaccination, to the public, and policy makers that will help them to further promote vaccinations, to control endemic, epidemic, and pandemic diseases.

There is a rapidly growing body of evidence, demonstrating that vaccination results significant and diverse health, economic, and social benefits, and increased herd protection. All of these, has resulted the enhanced ability to work long hours, productivity, enhanced cognitive function among healthy children, and potentially improved social equity.

Thus, instead of focusing on only health-centric benefits of vaccination, in measuring its impact, a broad social perspective, that allows us to measure economic and social benefits, is the appropriate standard, for health technology, and its products' assessment, in advancing the key perspectives, on the holistic benefits of vaccination in the society. Nonetheless, health-centric benefits are critical to mitigate health inequalities, through improving social equity, and promote social justice. Thus, vaccination drive must reach to under served populations, and hard-to-reach communities in the world.

Health benefits of vaccination

The traditional measures of vaccine include: vaccine efficacy (VE) as measured by the formula VE= $R_{unvaccinated}$-$R_{vaccinated}$/ $R_{vaccinated}$ where R=risk, under optimal conditions, such as trial settings. Thus, an effective numerical measure of vaccine impact, includes, estimation of prevention of disease transmission (in case of a infectious disease), the extent of morbidity, and mortality prevented. For example, in the United States, infectious diseases that largely accounted for substantial mortality and morbidity, in the early 20th century, showed over 90 per cent decline in incidence, by 2017, due to high vaccine uptake of over 90 per cent for DTP, MMR, and polio vaccines. In 2018, the global uptake of DTP reached 86 per cent that corresponded to 116,300,000 infants.

Another advantage of vaccination is the evidence that although vaccines may not always prevent an infection, such as VZB or pertussis, a milder disease course may follow. Vaccination greatly reduces disease, disability, death and inequality worldwide. Thus, the most significant impact of vaccines has been the marked reduction of infectious diseases morbidity, and mortality. Vaccines are estimated to prevent about six million deaths/year, and to save 386 million life years and 96 million disability-adjusted life years (DALYs), in the world. Thus, the potent impact of vaccination is the eradication of infectious diseases. For eradication of infectious diseases, high levels of population immunity are required globally, to prevent any human-to-human transmission of infection, in our well-connected world. India was declared polio free in 2014, through vaccination. Moreover, wild poliovirus type 2 was eradicated in 2015, and the wild type 3 was completely eradicated in 2019.

Vaccinations help to establish herd immunity in the population. When an adequate fraction of the population is vaccinated, transmission of the infectious agent is halted, that protects the unvaccinated ones those are too young, too susceptible, or too immunosuppressive to receive vaccines. Thus, herd (population) immunity, requires high levels of vaccine uptake, to reduce the number of unvaccinated people, and minimize the pathogen transmission, between vaccinated and unvaccinated ones. Interestingly, the proportion of a given population, for achieving herd immunity, through vaccination, is lower for the bacterial infections, as opposed to viral infections, due to lower R_0 for bacterial infection. Herd immunity has been observed for gastrointestinal infections, with vaccines against cholera (oral cholera vaccine), and rotavirus (oral rotavirus vaccine).

Another potential health benefit of vaccination is the reduction in secondary infections (opportunistic infections) that affect adversely vaccine-preventable diseases. Infections with pathogens, especially viruses, can increase the severity of disease by bacterial infections.

During the influenza pandemic of 1918-19, secondary bacterial bronchopneumonia with *S. pneumoniae, Streptococcus pyrogens, H. influenza,* and *Staphylococcus aureus,* identified at autopsy, presumably, resulted high mortality rates, observed among healthy children and adults.

Furthermore, there is evidence that inactivated influenza vaccines, given to pregnant women, can reduce the hospital admission, with acute respiratory illnesses, in their kids up to 6 months of age. Also, the introduction of live-attenuated measles vaccine, in the 1970s, was effective in reducing both measles, and non-measles mortality rates in children.

Also, historically, although, vaccines were developed to prevent infectious diseases, vaccines are being used to prevent non-communicable diseases, such as cancer, when the infectious agents are involved in carcinogenesis. For example, chronic hepatitis B infection can lead to liver cirrhosis, and hepatocellular carcinoma.

Moreover, the sexually transmitted HPV, that infects genital tract, and oropharyngeal tissue, causing cancer, in both men and women. The HPV serotypes 16 and 18, pose high-risk for cervical cancer, and vaccination against these specific serotypes are available, that are given to individuals, from the age of 9 years. Additional benefit of HPV vaccines is their beneficial effect on neonatal morbidity, and mortality. The cost efficiency of HPV vaccines is significantly underestimated, due to omission of conisation-associated prematurity, with neonatal mortality and morbidity.

A key example of "hidden" benefits of the vaccinations is the ability to reduce the morbidity, and mortality in the population, as a result of microbial resistance, to the multitude of antibiotics. The antimicrobial resistance is a serious threat, and leads to increasing the healthcare costs, longer duration of hospital stays, treatment failures, and deaths. Both viral and bacterial vaccines have the potential, to reduce the community's uptake of antibiotics. Reduction in antibiotic use, ranged from 5 to 10 per cent, in randomized controlled trials, up to relative reduction of 64 per cent, in epidemiological studies, indicating that vaccinations may reduce antibiotic utilization, and consequently, antibiotic resistance.

Economic benefits of vaccination

Vaccines are not only beneficial on a population level, but also cost-effective. Typically, national policymakers, and international organizations, commonly use the results of economic evaluation, in the context of health technology assessment, to make informed decisions, on vaccination programs.

However, many of the existing economic evaluations, tend to concentrate, on a narrow set of benefits, using a narrow perspective, including predominantly health gains, and medical cost savings, related to a disease, excluding other larger benefits, such as productivity gains, due to prevention of health deterioration, and associated mental disabilities. The reason is, in part, due to the fact that some of these larger benefits are "invisible" and/or difficult to quantify.

Thus, it is important to emphasize on key benefits of vaccination, that are typically neglected, in traditional economic evaluations, to assessing more accurately, the full value of vaccination. Frank G Sandmann and colleagues used an age-structured dynamic transmission, and economic model, to better understand, different scenarios of UK mass immunization programs, over 10 years. They were able to compare the vaccination data, from 75 per cent of individuals aged 15 years and older, 50 per cent of them (15 to 64 years) and 75 per cent of individuals, aged 65 years or older, who were either annually vaccinated to no vaccination. They assumed, either 50 per cent vaccine efficacy against disease, and 45-week protection (worst-case scenario) or 95 per cent vaccine efficacy, and 3-year protection (best-case scenario). Natural immunity was assumed to wane within 45 weeks. The QALYs and costs to both health care payers, and the national economy were measured. The data suggested that introducing vaccination led to incremental net monetary values ranging from 12.0 billion pounds to 33.7 billion pounds, in the best-case scenario, and from 1.1 billion pounds to 56.9 billion pounds, in the worst-case scenario. The cost-effectiveness analyses of vaccination programs tend to suggest, that they are worth the investment, as most programs costing less than $50 per life gained, that is much less than the health care spending, to manage hypertension. The returns on investment (ROI), in vaccines, have been estimated, to be at 12-18%, given their increasing provision through Gavi.

Federal survey data from the U.S. Census Bureau and National Center for Health Statistics indicate that vaccinations result immediate improvements in wellbeing. The vaccinated people feel less stress, such as feeling anxious, worried, low, or uninterested, most of the time. Reduced mental stress can minimize the possibility of developing physical ailments, such as hypertension, and cardiovascular diseases (CVDs). Moreover, less stressed people tend to be better at planning for the future, productive at work, and are able to take challenges. For example, according to the federal survey, conducted in the USA, between January 2021 and May 2021, 30 per cent of the people, who had at least one vaccine shot, reported being stressed, as opposed to 43.2 per cent of people, who were unvaccinated. The data is adjusted to disparities in income, race, ethnicities, or age. Thus, vaccination results significant improvement in mental health of the population.

Another important economic value of vaccination is productivity gain. As the relationship between health and the economy is bidirectional, that means economic growth enables increased funding, that in turn improve health; and a healthy population contributes more to the economy. Getting vaccinated leads to increased ability to safely return to work. For example, in March 2021, 52.4 of population in states, that had vaccinated, from 10 per cent to 30 per cent of the adults were working (americanprogress.com). Furthermore, in states that had vaccinated, from 30 per cent to 50 per cent of the adult population, 58.1 per cent people were working. In addition, healthy children show improved educational attainment at school, through better attendance, and better cognitive performance, after vaccination. With improved health, along with increased life expectancy, let families to invest more money, in the future, to enhance the education of the children, or through savings. Also, the economic impact of adult illness causes significant loss of productivity, for the duration of the illness, and the recovery period. The impact of childhood illness falls primarily on their adult caregivers, primarily, parents. Thus, when a child is sick that does not need hospital admission, the parent will have to forego their paid employment to take care of the child. In essence, vaccination programs should be considered as an investment in human, and collective social capital. Moreover, in low-income settings, improvement in children's survival, through vaccination, can potentially reduce fertility rates, as couples can reach their desired numbers of surviving children, with fewer pregnancies.

Additionally, the increased cost of child rearing, with rapid pace of economic development also contributes to fewer pregnancies. The reduced fertility provides a demographic dividend in the society, by minimizing the burden of youth dependency, and to augment living standards for their people. Moreover, community externalities are benefits, that spillover to unvaccinated people of the community, due to vaccinating the general population. These include protection from the infection, due to herd immunity together, with a reduction in antibiotic resistance, due to a decrease in the usage of antibiotic therapies.

Furthermore, cost-effective preparedness for future epidemic or pandemic outbreaks is one of the most important economic benefits of vaccination. Since, it is not feasible to predict the location, and the nature of the emerging threat, from an infectious disease, it is estimated that an investment of $4.5 billion/year in healthcare systems could potentially speed up responses to infectious epidemics, by prompt identification of the causative agent, and effective interventions, to limit the spread, and severity of the disease.

All things considered, the economic evaluation of vaccinations focuses primarily on three key aspects: First, the vaccine must be evaluated at the population level, instead of the subject level. Second, evaluation should be societal, as opposed to individual. Third, the period of evaluation should be well defined, linked to aims, such as disease-control, disease elimination, and/or disease eradication.

Social benefits of vaccination

Vaccination can have positive intergenerational effects, at the household level, by preventing premature disability or death among parents, and grandparents, who are caregivers for children. For example, human papillomavirus vaccination plays a significant role in lowering mortality rates among mothers. Moreover, at the population level, vaccination can reduce inequalities, and promote social equity, as it prevents diseases, that disproportionately affect those, who are socioeconomically disadvantaged.

Another important social benefit of vaccination is the strengthening of health, and social care infrastructure. For example, a successful vaccine program was proposed, in the Mission Indradhanush, in India, which aimed to make live-saving vaccines, for all children and pregnant women by 2020 through programs with national, state, district, and block/urban level input. Under this plan, states needed to obtain the vaccines, and store them appropriately, while eligible children were identified, through public health messaging, and outreach. Districts and urban areas recruited trained personnel, in vaccine delivery and communication, to administer vaccines and to provide post-care if required, which also provided basis for the provision of other health, and social care benefits to the communities. Also, empowerment of women, as a result of vaccination programs, is key to advancing the society. The degree of education, literacy, and freedom of females, varies considerably across the globe, and within countries. For example, in a case study, in the state of Bihar, in rural area, where women underwent an empowerment program, about health and hygiene, there was a higher rate of DTP, measles and BCG vaccination in their children, compared to the non-participants. Moreover, factors influencing the uptake of maternal vaccination, through empowerment programs, include women's previous experiences with healthcare, and a comprehensive knowledge about the nature of the vaccines, without any vaccine hesitancy and misinformation, that lets them to make informed choices, during the pregnancy.

The impact of vaccination on social policy: sustainable development goals

At the United Nations (UN) in New York, in 2015, the UN General Assembly proposed a set of global Sustainable Development Goals (SDGs), that comprises 17 goals and 169 targets, set out on a agenda, for sustainable development of all nations, that integrates economic growth, social inclusion, and environmental protection. They include no poverty, zero hunger, good health and wellbeing, quality education, and others. Interestingly, vaccination, directly impacts health (SDG3), and contributes to 14 out of the 17 SDGs, such as ending poverty, reducing hunger, and increasing social equity. The strength of the SDGs' universal call to action is clearly described in the design of its multicolored logo: a circle depicting how problems, and solutions are interconnected.

In many cases, vaccination bridges the different SDGs, and unifying these into a common solution. Vaccination is an excellent buying concept for the SDGs: a cost-effective public health intervention, whose benefits stretch far beyond its immediate impact (Gavi, the Vaccine Alliance), especially in low-to- middle-income countries (LMICs).

The ongoing COVID-19 pandemic puts the SDGs center stage, as by its very nature, a pandemic teaches that no one should be left behind, and that no one is safe, until everyone is safe. COVID-19 pandemic reminds us, why it is important to have a health insurance or access to healthcare, not having food or clean water supply during lockdowns, and importantly, not having civil rights-some of the goals, included under SDGs. With health as a lens, it is not difficult to understand, how the myriad targets incorporated into the SDGs are interlinked, and interdependent. Thus, how vaccination impacts directly or indirectly many of the SDGs, will be beneficial to policy makers, to promoting vaccination drives, around the world.

SDG1: No poverty

Globally, the number of people living in extreme poverty declined from 36 per cent in 1990 to 10 per cent in 2015. However, often, the pace of change decelerates, as a result of endemic, and pandemic diseases. A new research published by the UNU World Institute for Development Economics Research, warns, that the economic fallout from the worldwide pandemic, could increase global poverty by as much as half a billion people or 8 per cent of the world's population. As of now, more than 700 million people or 10 per cent of the world's population, still live in extreme poverty, struggling to fulfill the most basic needs, such as health, education, access to clean water and sanitation etc (UN.ORG). Prior to the ongoing COVID-19 pandemic, baseline projections tend to suggest that about 6 per cent of the global population, would be still living in extreme poverty, in 2030, clearly missing the deadline of ending poverty.

It is estimated, vaccines will have the greatest impact on reducing poverty, by combating hepatitis B helping an estimated 14 million people worldwide, avoid medical bankruptcy. Moreover, the measles vaccine is estimated to prevent about 22 million deaths.

A study from Harvard University, USA, co-authored by Gavi, the Vaccine Alliance, and its wide range of partners, modeled the health, and economic impact of vaccines for 10 diseases in 41 developing countries. This study shows that poorest 20 per cent of the population, included in the study, represented over a quarter of deaths, preventable by vaccination. Thus, it supports the notion that vaccination effectively reduces poverty introduced to developing countries. A vaccinated, healthy child is more likely to go to school, and become a more productive member of society in later life, and strengthens economies. Their families can also avoid the increased healthcare costs, due to diseases. Interestingly, for every USD 1 invested in vaccination in LMICs, there is an estimated $US 44 net benefit, to the overall economy, through longer, and healthier life.

SDG2: Zero hunger

After decades of steady decline, the number of people who suffer as a result of hunger, measured by the prevalence of undernourishment, began to slowly increase again, in 2015. If recent trends continue, the number of people affected by hunger would exceed 840 million by 2030.

Moreover, according to UN data, 2.37 billion people are without food or unable to eat a healthy balanced diet, on a regular basis. Thus, malnutrition is taking a heavy toll, across developing, and developed nations.

Vaccination, and good nutrition are important for healthier children and families. Malnourished children are more prone to die from infectious disease due to weaker immunity. Many of the deaths are prevented by effective immunization against diseases, such as pneumonia, diarrhea, and measles. Malnutrition is not only caused by a lack of nutritious food, as many infectious diseases, such as diarrhea and malaria can cause under-nutrition, by reducing body's ability, to absorb nutrients. Thus, preventing infectious disease, through vaccination, is critical for child health, and development.

SDG3: Good health and well-being

Sustainable Development Goal 3 seeks to ensure health, and wellbeing for all, at every stage of life. The goal addresses all major health priorities, that include maternal, and child health, communicable and non-communicable diseases, universal health coverage, and effective, quality and affordable medicines, and vaccines.

Importantly, it aims for more research and development, focusing on health risk reduction, and management. Vaccination helps to achieve many of the SDG3 targets, such as reduction of maternal mortality (Target 3.1), end all preventable deaths under 5 (Target 3.2), fight communicable diseases (Target 3.3), reduce mortality from non-communicable diseases, such as cancer, and promote mental health (Target 3.4).

Today, vaccines save 2-3 million lives every year, and millions more are protected from disease, and disability. Millions of children are alive, and healthy, as a result of vaccination. Vaccination periodically reaches more households than any other health service, and brings communities into regular contact with the healthcare system. Thus, it essentially provides, ideal platform, to deliver other primary healthcare services, and upon which to build universal health coverage.

Bogler and colleagues estimated the effect of measles vaccination on child growth, using Demographic and Health Surveys (DHS), covering the period from 1990 to 2017. Stunting, wasting, and underweight are targets used to assess progress, towards the achievement of SDGs. In this study, the authors, controlled for a wide-range of confounders, such as sex, age, birth order, and mother's age at birth, as well as, vaccination with DPT and others. Measles vaccination was associated with significantly reduced odds of stunting (odds ratio 0.90 (95% CI 0.86-0.94), P<0.001), and underweight (odds ratio 0.90(95% CI 0.86-0.95), p<0.001). However, the association with wasting is weaker, and not statistically significant (odds ratio 0.95 (95% CI 0.89-1.02), p<0.143). Thus, measles vaccination, substantially reduces stunting and underweight, among children in LMIC, and boosts child growth, and the attainment of good health and wellbeing.

SDG4: Quality education

Sustainable Development Goal 4 is essentially the education goal. It aims to ensure inclusive and equitable quality education, and promote lifelong learning opportunities for all.

Vaccination is helpful in achieving 10 targets, under SDG4, by improving learning ability, of the children. Vaccination improves educational attainment in the kids, as vaccinated ones are able to go to school, and perform better, that positively impact cognitive development, as well as, long-term productivity. Furthermore, schools are a good platform for health promotion, delivery of vaccines, and other necessary health services. The children of educated parents have a greater chance of being vaccinated, and well nourished and thus enjoy better health.

SDG5: Gender equality

Immunization/vaccination is essentially empowering women and girls. Human papillomavirus (HPV) vaccines are effective in preventing most cervical cancers (70%) among adolescent girls. Thus, they have a demographic dividend of better women's health, in the next generation, especially in developing countries (Kristen Kelleher, Gavi). Interestingly, more than 85 per cent of deaths, as a result of cervical cancer, occur in LMIC.

Furthermore, vaccination is a gender-equal intervention. Girls and boys are immunized at the similar rates, worldwide. Gavi supports a wide range of countries, to make focused efforts to identify, and address gender-related hurdles to immunization services, through training programs for female healthcare professionals, as empowering women is critical to the expand the child vaccination coverage.

SDG6: Clean water and sanitation

Every year millions of people, especially the children, die from infectious diseases, associated with inadequate clean water supply, sanitation, and hygiene. Between 1990 and 2015, the proportion of the global population, using an improved drinking water source, increased from 76 per cent to 91 per cent. However, about 1000 children die every day, due to water, and sanitation-related diarrheal diseases.

According to the World Bank, more than 520 million people in India are defecating in the open-the highest number in the world. Thus, improving sanitation is a key priority of the Government of India that has introduced several flagship programs, such as Swachh Bharat Abhiyan, the National Rural Drinking Water Program, and Namami Gange, which aims at the conservation of the River Ganga. Vaccines, along with clean water, sanitation and hygiene (WASH), are proven interventions, to prevent diarrheal diseases, a leading cause of child morbidity, and mortality in LMICs. Moreover, investment in oral cholera and rotavirus vaccines, WASH, and health systems, using an integrated approach, is key to completely eliminating diarrheal diseases.

SDG7: Affordable and clean energy

Sustainable Development Goal 7 aims to ensure access to affordable, reliable, sustainable, and modern energy for all. Energy is central to nearly every major challenge, and opportunity the world faces today, including, poverty eradication, gender equality, and adaptation to climate change, food security, health, education, jobs, and transport etc.

Vaccination programs, and their modernization, in terms of technology and equity, bring newer, cleaner and more affordable means, to developing countries' health system. For example, Gavi's cold chain equipment optimization platform, provides access, to solar, and energy efficient refrigeration, that is cost-effective, and environment friendly. Additionally, Gavi's supports, include, vaccine-tracking system, that ensures optimum energy usage, and reduce wastage. Vaccination drive can accelerate progress on energy access, in poorer countries, such as Africa, where about 600 million people, across the continent still lack reliable electricity. Pandemic responses, and figuring out better strategies for vaccines distribution can potentially bridge the crippling access gap in the population.

SDG8: Decent work and economic Growth

In essence, healthy population leads to more productive workforce. Investment in human, and social capital can potentially strengthen a country's competiveness, towards achieving its sustainable goals.

Thus, Sustainable Development Goal 8 aims to ensure an economic growth rate of 7 per cent, for the least developed countries by 2030, and achieve decent employment, for all men and women everywhere in the world, in the next 15 years.

The flagship programs, such as National Skill Development Mission, Deendayal Upadhaya Antodaya Yojana, Atal Innovation

Mission, National Service Scheme, and Mahatma Gandhi National Rural Employment Guarantee Scheme, introduced by the Government of India, are aimed at bringing decent works for all.

Thus, in order to boost country's competitiveness in achieving key goals, it is important to have a productive workforce, by improving its health, through vaccination. In addition, vaccinated healthy children, free up parents' time, so that are able to work. Interestingly, in Gavi-supported countries, every USD 1 spent on immunization, typically generates USD 54, in broader societal benefits, that let population to live longer, and provide quality lives.

SDG9: Industry, innovation, and infrastructure

Sustainable Development Goal 9 ensures building resilient infrastructure; promote inclusive and sustainable industrialization, and foster innovation. Thus, they essentially play a key role, in introducing new technologies, facilitating and unifying international trade, and enabling the efficient use of resources, across the globe.

The pandemics in the past, and the present revealed the urgent need for resilient infrastructure. Moreover, pandemics, typically hit hard the manufacturing industries, and causes disruption in global value chains, and supply of the key products, such as vaccines. Gavi makes vaccine markets function better, by attracting more suppliers, resulting reduction of vaccine prices, and ensuring more equitable and sustainable access to life saving vaccines, and other innovative products, that meet developing countries' needs. Innovative new vaccines, such as vaccine, against Ebola virus, can prevent pandemics, before they start, and better prepare the world for disease outbreak, and thus, help fulfilling SGD goals. The fast-track development of the Ebola vaccine, contributed to the effective development of vaccine manufacturing infrastructure, and innovative vaccine distribution platforms.

SDG10: Reduced inequalities

Sustainable Development Goal 10 aims at reduction in inequalities, and ensuring no one is left behind, which is integral to achieving the SDGs. Inequalities are more prevalent, in countries for vulnerable people, with weaker health systems, and those facing existing humanitarian crises. Moreover, a pandemic exacerbates inequalities, affecting primarily, the women and girls. Thus, challenging the existing health systems is essentially testing our common humanity.

Also, vaccination protects the health of the communities, reduces the number of people forced into poverty, and gives a growing child an equal chance of a healthier, and more prosperous future. Thus, better health, leads to increased equality. By concentrating more on the underserved communities, and the children of the unvaccinated ("zero dose"), underserved communities, especially, those belong to marginalized populations, living in remote rural and conflict areas, Gavi brings vaccination, and primary healthcare services to those who are left behind, and needed most.

SDG11: Sustainable cities and communities

Sustainable Development Goal 11 aims to make cities and human settlements inclusive, safe, resilient, and sustainable.

Rapid urbanization over years is resulting in a growing number of slum dwellers, overburdened infrastructure, and key public services, such as waste collection, water and sanitation systems, roads and transport. Half of the world population (3.5 billion) lives in the cities today, and 5 billion people are projected to live in cities by 2030.

Thus, by 2030, 70 per cent of the global population is predicted to live in urban settlements. Effective immunization always leads to healthier cities. Strengthening urban immunization programs protects the enormous population in urban areas against the risk of infectious disease outbreaks, and also provides opportunity for integrated preventive services, to cover urban and underserved communities.

SDG13: Climate action

Sustainable Development Goal 13 aims to take urgent action to combat climate change, and its impact.

The impact of climate change on public health is enormous, that cuts across wellbeing, livelihood, and social security of people, especially, for the poorest and most vulnerable communities, such as people on the move. Many of the infectious disease outbreaks happen due to climate changes, such as yellow fever, cholera and Ebola, specifically in urban, and weak post-disaster settings. Thus, vaccination is critical to building people's trust on health systems, and reducing the emergence of infectious diseases.

SDG16: Peace, justice and strong Institutions

In essence, strong health systems provide long-term stability in the society. Conflict, insecurity, weak institutions, and limited access to justice pose a great threat to sustainable development. By respecting human rights, such as access to life saving vaccines, especially, at the time of crisis, it is possible, to build more effective and inclusive solutions of today, and recovery for tomorrow. The best response is one that responds adequately to immediate threats, and simultaneously protects the human rights and the rule of law. Effective, safe, and strong people-centric health systems, are the backbone of social institutions of every country.

Vaccination is often the first point of contact between these systems and the population. The role of Gavi is critical in this aspect, to improve vaccine equity, that further helps to building public trust, greater social cohesion, peaceful, and inclusive society.

SDG17: Partnership for the goals

Leveraging the comparative advantage of each partner, the innovative public-private partnership model, conceived by the Vaccine Alliance, has been advancing the global progress, by accelerating the equitable, and sustainable access to multitude of vaccines, both, as scale and pace. This partnership model has helped to reduce mortality rate, from vaccine-preventable diseases, by more than 60 per cent, and also played a major role in reducing the under-five mortality rate in those countries. Thus, innovative partnership models lead to unprecedented progress in achieving one of the key goals of sustainable development.

Taken together, the most critical need of the hour is to develop a universal preparedness for health, in tune, with the spirit of the SDGs. Health must be assessed in the broadest of contexts, with utmost attention to social structures, infrastructures, along with strategies, to counteract climate change. The 'oneness of humanity' as a result of vaccination drive, across the world, will only brighten our ability to achieve majority of the SDGs and it's "forest of targets". It is also important that broader benefits of vaccination need to be accurately estimated, in evaluation methods, including economic models, used currently. Without fully exploiting the broad benefits of vaccination, with interconnected effects among SGDs, it is difficult to successfully implement SDGs in the society. Renewed emphasis on the importance of social policy, such as SDGs, in the context of worldwide vaccination drive, during COVID-19 pandemic, will advance the society to an enormous extent.

Figure 25. The different Sustainable Development Goals.

Source: United Nations.

Figure 26. The impact of vaccines in terms of health, economic, and social benefits.

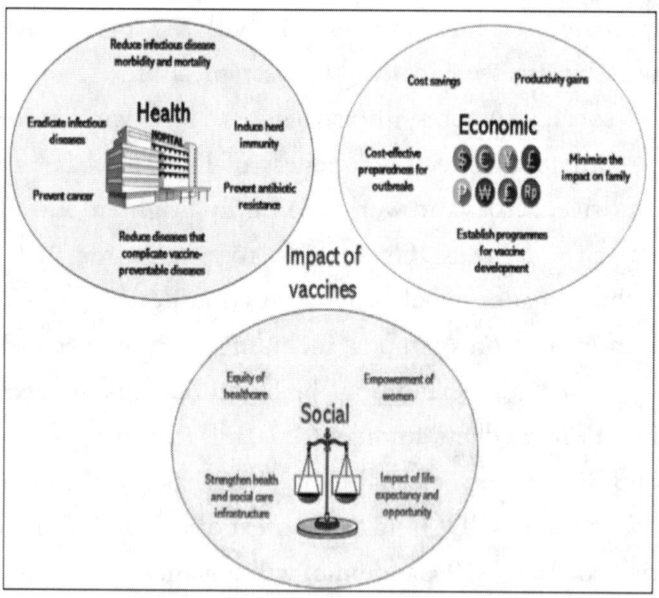

Source: Front Microbiol. 2020. 11-1526

References

Vaccines. S.A. Plotkin and E.A. Mortimer. Philadelphia, W.B Saunders Co. ISBN 07216658459780721665849.

The global value of vaccination. J. Ehreth. *Vaccine.* 2003 Jan 30; 21(7-8): 596-600. DOI: https://doi.org/10.1016/s0264-410x(02)00623-0.

United Nations Department of Economic and Social Affairs. Economic Analysis. 2019. https://www.un.org/development/desa/dpad/tag/2019/

Impact of vaccines; Health, Economic and Social Perspectives. M.C. Charlene et al. *Front. Microbiol.*, 14 July 2020. DOI: https://doi.org/10.3389/fmicb.2020.01526).

The Societal Value of Vaccination in the Age of COVID-19. D. E. Bloom et al. *Am J Public Health.* 2021 June; 111(6): 1049-1054. DOI: https://doi.org/10.2105/AJPH.2020.306114).

Vaccine effects and impact of vaccination programmes in post-licensure studies. G. Hanquet et al. *Vaccine*, 31 (2013), pp 5634-5642. DOI: https://doi.org/10.1016/j.vaccine.2013.07.006)

The vaccine effectiveness: the direct or indirect effect of vaccinations on the population in a real-life setting. Charloner-Larsson G. Training manual on the critical regulatory function for vaccines: evaluation of clinical performance through authorized clinical trials: prepared for national regulatory authorities of vaccine-procuring and vaccine-producing countries, WHO/V&B/03.12: 2003.

World Health Organization (2019b). *Immunization coverage*, Geneva: World Health Organization.

Vaccination greatly reduces disease, disability, death and inequality worldwide. F.E. Andre et al. *Bull. World Health Organ.* 2008 February; 86(2): 140-6. DOI: https://doi.org/10.2471/blt.07.040089.

The intangible benefits of vaccination-what is the true economic value of vaccination? P. Bonanni et al. *J. Mark. Access Health Policy.* 2015;3:10.3402/jmahp.v3.26964. DOI: https://doi.org/3:10.3402/jmahv3.26964.

Vaccination greatly reduces disease, disability, death, and inequality worldwide. F.E. Andre et al. *Bull World Health Organ.* 2008, 86, 140-146. DOI: https://doi.org/10.2471/BLT.07.040089.

The 1918 influenza pandemic: insights for the 21st century. D.M. Morens and A.S. Fauci. *J. Infect. Dis.* 2007 Apr 1; 195(7): 1018-28. DOI: https://doi.org/10.1086/511989.

Effect of Maternal Influenza Vaccination on Hospitalization for Respiratory Infections in Newborns: A Retrospective Cohort study. A.K. Regan et al. *Pediatr. Infect. Dis.* 2016 Oct; 35(10) :1097-103. DOI: https://doi.org/10.1097/INF.0000000000001258.

Y. Bogler et al. "Epidemiology and natural history of chronic hepatitis B virus infection," in *Hepatitis B Virus and Liver Disease,* Eds J.H. Kao and D.S. Chen (Berlin: Springer), 2018, 63-89.

Impact of vaccines on antimicrobial resistance. P. Buchy et al. Int J Infect Dis. 2020 Jan; 90:188-196. DOI: https://doi.org/10.1016/j.jiid.2019.10.005.

Involvement of human papillomaviruses in cervical cancer. Wang, X. et al. *Front. Microbiol.*2018, 9:2896. DOI: https://doi.org/10.3389/fmich.2018.02896

HPV vaccines: global perspectives. G. Gupta et al. *Hum. Vacc. Immunotherap.* 2017, 13, 1-4. DOI: https://doi.org/10.1080/21645515.2017.1289301.

A review of the effect of immunization programs on antimicrobial utilization. K.J. Wilby and D. Werry. *Vaccine.* 2012; 30(46): 6509-14. DOI: https://doi.org/10.1016/j.vaccine.2012.08.031.

The societal value of vaccination in developing countries. A.E. Shearley. *Vaccine* Oct 29; 17, Suppl.3: S109-12. DOI: https://doi.org/10.1016/s0264-410x(99)00303-5.

D. E. Bloom et al. et al. The Value of Vaccination. *World Econ.* Vol. 6. No. 3. July-September 2005. https://www.world-economics-journal.com/The%20Value%20of%20Vaccination.details?AID=213.

The potential health and economic value of SARS-CoV-2 vaccination alongside physical distancing in the UK: a transmission model-based future scenario analysis and economic evaluation. F. G Sandmann et al. *The Lancet Infectious Diseases,* Vol. 21, Issue 7, July 2021, P962-974. DOI: https://doi.org/10.1016/S1473-3099(21)00079-7.

The broader economic impact of vaccination: reviewing and appraising the strength of evidence. M. Jit et al. *BMC Medicine.* 13. 209 (2015). DOI: https://doi.org/10.1186/s12916-015-0446-9.

Africa's prospects for enjoying a demographic dividend. D.E. Bloom et al. *J Demogr Economics.* 2017; 83(1): 63-76.

Role of vaccination in the sustainability of healthcare systems. N. Largeron et al. *Journal of Market Access Health Policy.* 2015; 3:10.3402/jmahp.v3.27043. DOI: https://doi.org/10.3402/jmahp.v3.27043.

GHRF Commission (2016). *Commission on a Global Health Risk Framework for the Future. The Neglected Dimension of Global Security A Framework to Counter Infectious Disease Crisis. Commission on Global Health Framework for the Future.* https://nam.edu/wp-content/uploads/2016/01/Neglected-Dimension-of-Global-security.pdf).

How is the economic assessment of vaccines performed today? *J Mark Access Health Policy.* 2017; 5(1): 1335163. DOI: https://doi.org/10.1080/20016689.2017.1335163).

Economic evaluation of vaccination: capturing the full benefits, with an application to human papillomavirus. T. Barnighausen et al. *Clin Microbiol Infect.* 2012; 18: 70-76. DOI: https://doi.org/10.1111/j.1469-0691.2012.03977.x.).

The Societal Value of Vaccination in the Age of COVID-19.Bloom D.E. Bloom et al. *Am J Public Health.* 2021 June; 111(6): 1049-1054. DOI: https://doi.org/10.2015/AJPH.2020.306114).

Immunization equity. A.R. Hinman A.R and M.A. Mckinlay. *Am J Prev Med.* 2015. Dec: 49(6 Suppl 4): S399-405. DOI: https://doi.org/10.1016/j.amepre.2015.04.018.

Externalities in program evaluation: The impact of a Women's empowerment program on immunization. W. Jenssens. August 2011. Journal of European Economic Association 9(6): 1082-1113. DOI: https://doi.org/10.1111/j.1542-4774.2011.01041.x

Strategies to improve maternal vaccination acceptance. Wilson R et al. 2019 *BMC Public Health* 19:342. DOI: https://doi.org/10.1186/s12889-019-6655-y.

Advancing sustainability science for the SDGs. M. Stafford-Smith et al. November 2018. *Sustainability Science* 13(4). DOI: https://doi.org/10.1007/s11625-018-0645-3.

Weisenborn Gerg, "United nations Sustainable Development Goals" (2018). *Times Talk Archive.* 81. https://scholars.fhsu.edu/times_talk_archive/81).

Achieving The Sustainable Development Goals: six reasons why immunisation matters. K. Kelleher, *Gavi, the Vaccine Alliance.*

COVID-19 puts the Sustainable Development Goals center stage. O.P. Ottersen and E. Engebretsen. *Nature Medicine* 26, 1672-1673 (2020). DOI: https://doi.org/10.1038/s41591-020-1094-y).

Policy: Map the interactions between Sustainable Development Goals. M. Nilsson et al. *Nature* 534, 320-322(2016). DOI: https://doi.org/10.1038/534320a

https://UNSTATS.UN.ORG/SDGS/REPORT/2020/).

(https://www.gavi.org/our-alliance/global-health-development/sustainable-development-goals.

Estimating the effect of measles vaccination on child growth using 191 DHS from 65 Low- and middle-income countries. L. Bogler et al. *Vaccine,* Vol. 37, Issue 35, 2019, P 5073-5088. DOI: https://doi.org/10.1016/j.vaccine.2019.06.054.

COVID-19: Why Declining Biodiversity Puts Us at Greater Risk for Emerging Infectious Diseases, and What We Can Do. A.K. Khetan. *J.Gen.Intern.Med.* 2020 Sep; 35(9): 2746-2747. DOI: https://doi.org/10.1007/s11606-020-05977-x.

Reset Sustainable Development Goals for a pandemic world. R. Naidoo and B. Fisher. *Nature* July 2020. https://www.nature.com/articles/d41586-020-01999-x.

The COVID-19 Vaccination Drive: An Indian Update

> "Inequalities in health have always existed, but at this moment there is an awakening to the power of racism, poverty and bias in amplifying the health and economic pain and hardship imposed by this [COVID-19] pandemic."
>
> – Helene Gayle

> "India surpasses 1bn vaccine mark after stuttering start to campaign.'
>
> – Financial Times

> "It brings me great pride that COVISHIELD is part of this historic effort & to endorse its safety & efficacy, I join our health workers in taking the vaccine myself."
>
> – Adar Poonawalla

Social inequality refers to relational process in society that has the effect of limiting or harming a group's social status, social class, and social circle. One of the key components of social inequality is health inequality that is dependent on the socioeconomic, and cultural disparities in the population. Thus, one of the key aspects of the Sustainable Development Goals (SDGs) is the attainment of good health, and wellbeing (SDG3) in the general population. Social inequality often leads to disparities in the distribution of health-related benefits, and also, the quality of the healthcare.

Moreover, social inequality leading to health disparities in the population, results from the inequalities in the social capital-knowledge gain, through personal, and community network. Thus, health policies that promote social capital building along all sections of society, is beneficial for improved healthcare access, that in turn strengthens a society's response to any emerging pandemic.

Universal vaccination across the world, stems from the urgent necessity of protecting people, belong to all socioeconomic classes from an infectious disease, by preventing transmission of infections from the most vulnerable, and healthcare deprived section of the society. Thus, essentially, universal vaccination programs remove the social inequality, such as health inequalities, through building social capital, by developing vaccine awareness, and knowledge in the population, and further negating economic disparities, by providing free access of vaccination to the population, who may not be able to afford it.

A pandemic situation gives all of us a chance to better understand the consequence of socioeconomic, and cultural disparities that exist in the society, and the importance of vaccination not only in preventing the transmission of the infectious disease, and its severity, but, also introduces cohesion in the society, that is key to working together, towards other common goals, in the true spirit of SDGs.

A year and half has passed since the appearance of the first case of novel coronavirus (SARS-CoV-2) in China's Wuhan province. Over the entire 2020, the efforts were primarily concentrated on preventing, and slowing the disease transmission, using largely non-pharmacological interventions, when the development of COVID-19 vaccines were underway. However, the worldwide analysis of herd immunity, during this time, has indicated insufficient herd immunity, acquired by the people, emphasizing the need to develop effective vaccines, and establish vaccine-induced immunity in the population, to prevent further spread of disease transmission. Also, recent evidence tend to suggest that people with previous SARS-CoV-2 infection, elicits unusually potent immune responses (25 to 100 times higher antibody response) to COVID-19 vaccines, due to hybrid immunity, driven by memory B cells and CD4 (+) T cells, and broader cross-protection from COVID-19 variants. Moreover, natural immunity developed through natural SARS-CoV-2 infection, wanes overtime that further supports the notion of hybrid immunity. Thus, despite, amid anti-vaccination movements in many parts of the world, based on solid scientific evidence, it is absolutely critical to get vaccinated, and develop a long-term protection against COVID-19 disease.

India rolled out the world's largest vaccination drive on January 16, 2021 to vaccinate about 300 million priority groups, against COVID-19 diseases. India has granted emergency use authorization (EUA) to two made-in-India COVID-19 vaccines on January 3, 2021. The initial plan was to cover about 300 million priority groups, who are at increased risk of getting infected with COVID-19 virus, that included 10 million healthcare professionals, 20 million frontline workers, and about 270 million people above age 50 years and/or with co-morbidities. However, due to unanticipated, devastating second wave of COVID-19 pandemic over the month of April 2021 to June 2021, a universal vaccination program using the two made-in-India vaccines was launched in April 2021, to cover all age groups, including children. According to the International Air Transport Association (IATA), it would require thousands of flights to bring the foreign-made vaccines, from the production sites abroad, to the distribution sites in India. However, due to acute, larger demand of vaccine doses, in the middle of worst second wave of COVID-19 pandemic,

Government of India decided to buy foreign vaccines, such as Sputnik V, and also has laid the foundation for key collaborations with overseas vaccine manufactures, such as Pfizer-BioNTech and Moderna (USA), Sputnik V (Russia), Johnson & Johnson (UK) (single-dose vaccine) to produce these vaccines indigenously, in partnership with private Indian vaccine manufacturing companies. Additionally, there are few others made-in-India vaccines in the pipeline, for example, DNA vaccine from Zydus- Cadila, and protein vaccine 'Corbevax', developed by Indian biopharmaceutical firm Biological E. Limited, in collaboration with Baylor College of Medicine, U.S., and company Dynavax Technologies, U.S. Since, India's vaccine supply chains have already been tried and tested with the rollout of two homemade vaccines, it is expected that a massive vaccine rollout program with other types of vaccines available in the country, over a short period to time, with the help of previously trained personnel and vaccine coordinators, will cover a majority of the 1.4 billion population for full-dose vaccination.

As of October 25, 2021, India has administered 71,84,44,141 single-dose (70% of population) and 30,57,05,808 (30% of population) full-dose COVID-19 vaccine, since the beginning of the vaccination drive on January 16, 2021. The number of nationwide COVID-19 confirmed caseload, at the peak of the second wave on May 1, 2021, was 19,549,775. The recoveries, and deaths were 15,981,938 and 215,524 respectively. As of October 18, 2021, the number of nationwide COVID-19 conformed caseload was 34,081,315. The recoveries, and deaths were 33,439,331 and 452,290 respectively. Therefore, between May 1, 2021 and October 18, 2021, there has been a 1.74-fold increase of COVID-19 caseload in the country. The ratio of total caseload and number of recoveries was about 1.23 on May 1, 2021 and 1.01 on October 18, 2021. Thus, it appears that vaccination seems to increase the recovery rate of the COVID-19 patients marginally, during this period, and also keeps the fold-increase in COVID-19 caseload to a minimum. The data is striking, considering the fact that only about 30% per cent of the population was fully vaccinated during this period.

The cumulative COVID-19 caseload across India from January 30, 2000 to October 18, 2021 was over 34 million. The death rate, as defined by the total number of deaths divided by total number of COVID-19 caseload, was 0.011 on May 1, 2021 compared to 0.012 on October 18, 2021. Therefore, vaccination seems to minimize the enormous death rates, and new infections, observed in the Indian society, during the peak of the second wave, in early May 2021. More data is needed, in terms of rate of hospitalization, duration of the stay in the hospital, case fatality rate, morbidity, and mortality rate, for better assessment about the effectiveness of the vaccines in the population. The duration of protection from new COVID-19 infection and/or re-infections (breakthroughs), as a result of vaccination, is also another key measurement that needs to be evaluated in a longitudinal study in COVID-19 patients, by comparing infection data on vaccinated individuals, and unvaccinated ones. Furthermore, comparison between COVID-19-related hospitalization rates and death rates, in vaccinated population with unvaccinated individuals, is also critical parameters, that need to be addressed, to better understand the correlation between vaccination numbers and the reduction in the severity of COVID-19 caseloads, among the India population. Thus, periodic updates on the vaccination data, and associated primary clinical outcomes measurement, such as symptomatic COVID-19 cases, hospitalization rates, length of hospitalization stay, case fatality rates, and mortality rates in COVID-19 patients, together with secondary clinical outcomes measurement, such as long COVID symptoms (mild symptoms that stay over a longer period of time), and frequency of follow up patients' visits to clinics after hospital discharge, will further help clinicians, to come up with better decision about the vaccination approach, and its necessary amendments.

The daily doses in COVID-19 vaccines administered, to people in rural and urban areas, as of July 15, 2021, indicated that, although, the people belong to rural area had received larger doses of vaccines, compared to people in urban areas, the proportion of vaccine doses administered to them had been less than the urban population, since rural population is more in India compared to urban population. As urban population has always been affected more since the beginning of the COVID-19 pandemic, it is important to get them fully vaccinated quickly, to prevent the further spread of disease transmission. Moreover, the vaccination rate has been lower in rural areas, as people are skeptical about its benefit, due to misinformation. Also, women are vaccinated about 16 per cent less compare to Indian men as per BBC (British Broadcasting Company) report on India's vaccination drive.

In addition, it would take about additional 1.8 billion doses to vaccinate all eligible adults in India as per BBC report. The projected availability of five vaccines: 500 million doses of Covishield, 400 million doses of Covaxin, 300 million doses of a vaccine from Biological E, 100 million doses from Sputnik V, and 50 million doses of ZyCov-Di, being developed by Zydus-Cadila. The top five Indian states, in terms or cumulative number of COVID-19 doses administered, as of October 25, 2021, are Uttar Pradesh (125,463.01), Maharashtra (95,279.77), West Bengal (72,070.7), Gujarat (68,712.05), and Madhya Pradesh (68,566.71).

The state of Maharashtra, Karnataka, Andhra Pradesh, and Kerala are the highest COVID-19 affected, since the beginning of the pandemic. As of October 18, 2021, the number of vaccines administered in these four states 91,434,37, 60,895,16, 46,697,16, and 37,250,74 respectively. The number of COVID-19 confirmed cases across these states, as of October 18, 2021, are 6,591,697 (Maharashtra), 2,983,459 (Karnataka), 2,060,472 (Andhra Pradesh), and 4,854,321 (Kerala). It would be unwise to make any correlation between vaccination numbers and the infection cases, as other parameters, that might affect infection transmission, have not been taken into account. For example, the vaccination numbers are relatively close for the state of Andhra Pradesh and Kerala (46,697,16 versus 37,250,74). However, the confirmed COVID-19 caseloads are 2.36-fold higher, in the state of Kerala (4,854,321), as opposed to Andhra Pradesh (2,060,472).

Importantly, more granular analyses on vaccination data across the country, dissecting the socioeconomic, and cultural groups in the population including transgender; others, as per COWIN (COVID Vaccine Intelligence Work), is needed to better understand the health inequalities in the Indian society, and how vaccination program can effectively mitigate the disparities.

Figure 27. The underlying mechanism of hybrid vigor immunity in the individuals: Previously infected individuals with SARS-CoV-2 when vaccinated develop robust hybrid immunity against the COVID-19 disease. This hybrid vigor immunity results from a synergy between naturally induced and vaccine-induced immunity. In analogy to hybrid vigor in plants, when natural immunity to SARS-CoV-2 is combined with vaccine-generated immunity, a larger-than-expected immune response arises that is primarily mediated by the memory B- and T-lymphocytes. Memory B cells produce identical antibodies upon re-infection with the same virus, and encode a library of antibody mutations, a stockpile of immunological variants as evolutionary strategy. These diverse memory B cells provide the immune system the ability to fight against emerging viral variants. Hybrid vigor immunity results 25 to 100 times higher antibody responses and also provides broader cross-protection from SARS-CoV-2 variants.

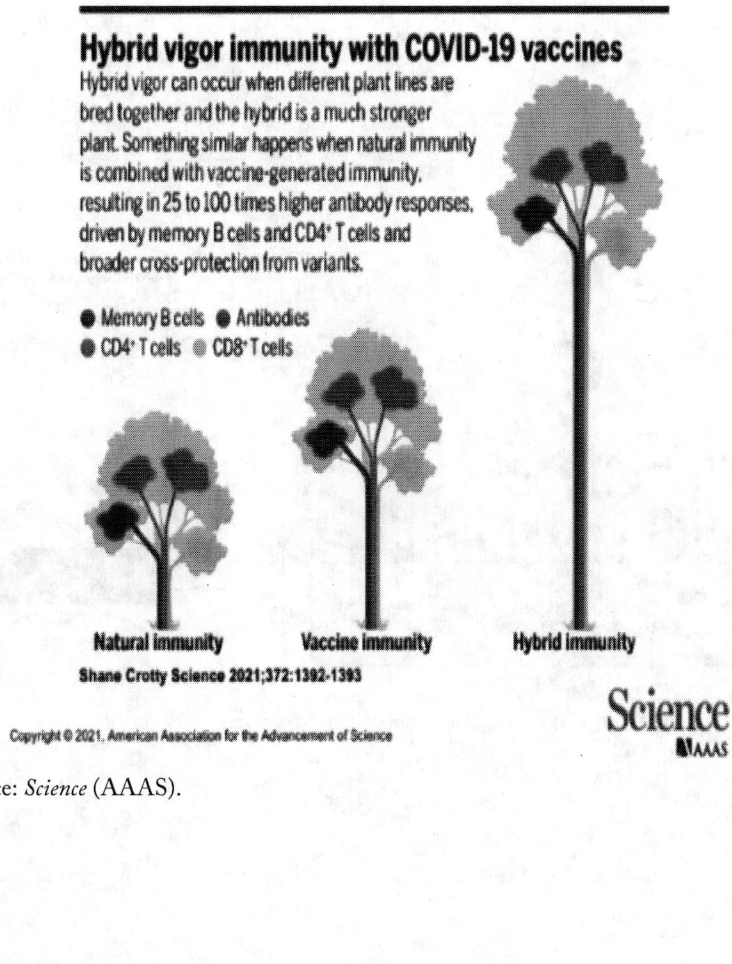

Source: *Science* (AAAS).

Figure 28. India's vaccination drive: **(A),** Total number of COVID-19 vaccine doses administered till October 19, 202, **(B),** Share of Indians who received at least one dose of COVID-19 vaccine **(C),** Share of Indian population fully vaccinated against COVID-19 **(D),** Daily doses of COVID-19 vaccine administered in rural and urban India till July 15, 2021 **(E),** Number of COVID-19 vaccine doses administered in India as of October 25, 2021.

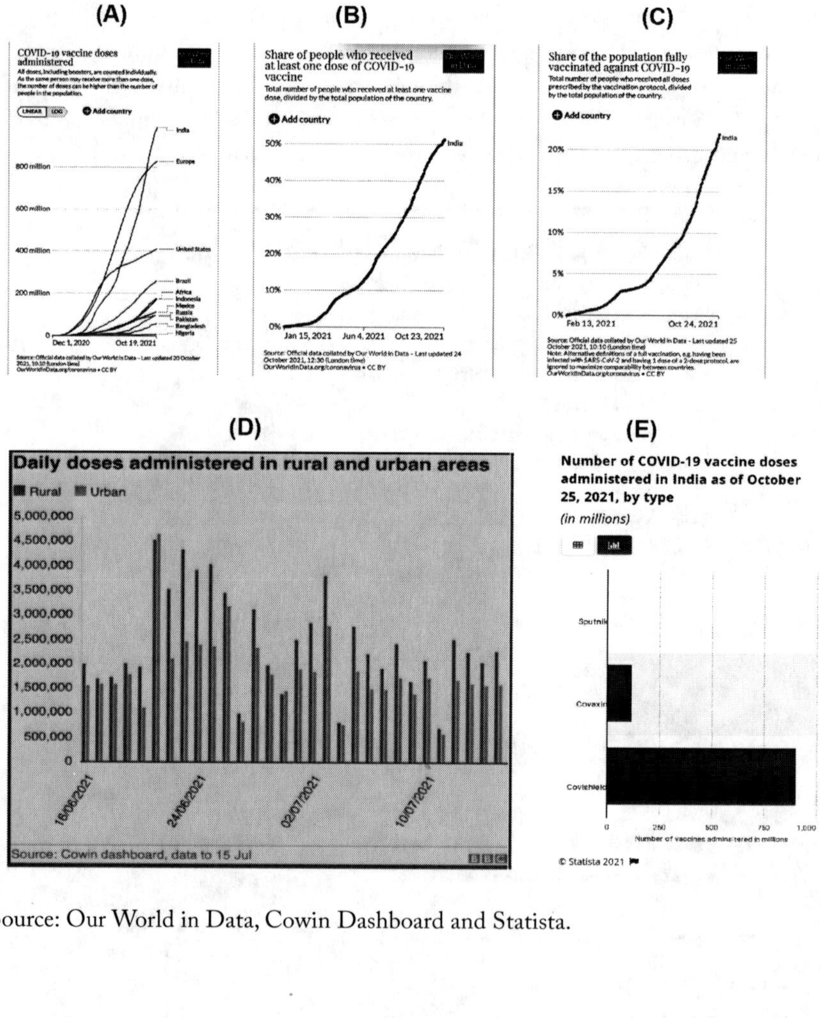

Source: Our World in Data, Cowin Dashboard and Statista.

Figure 29. COVID-19 cases across India: **(A)** Cumulative conformed COVID-19 cases as of October 24, 2021 **(B)** Daily new conformed COVID-19 cases till October 24, 2001 **(C)** Age-stratified number of COVID-19 cases as of October 18, 2021.

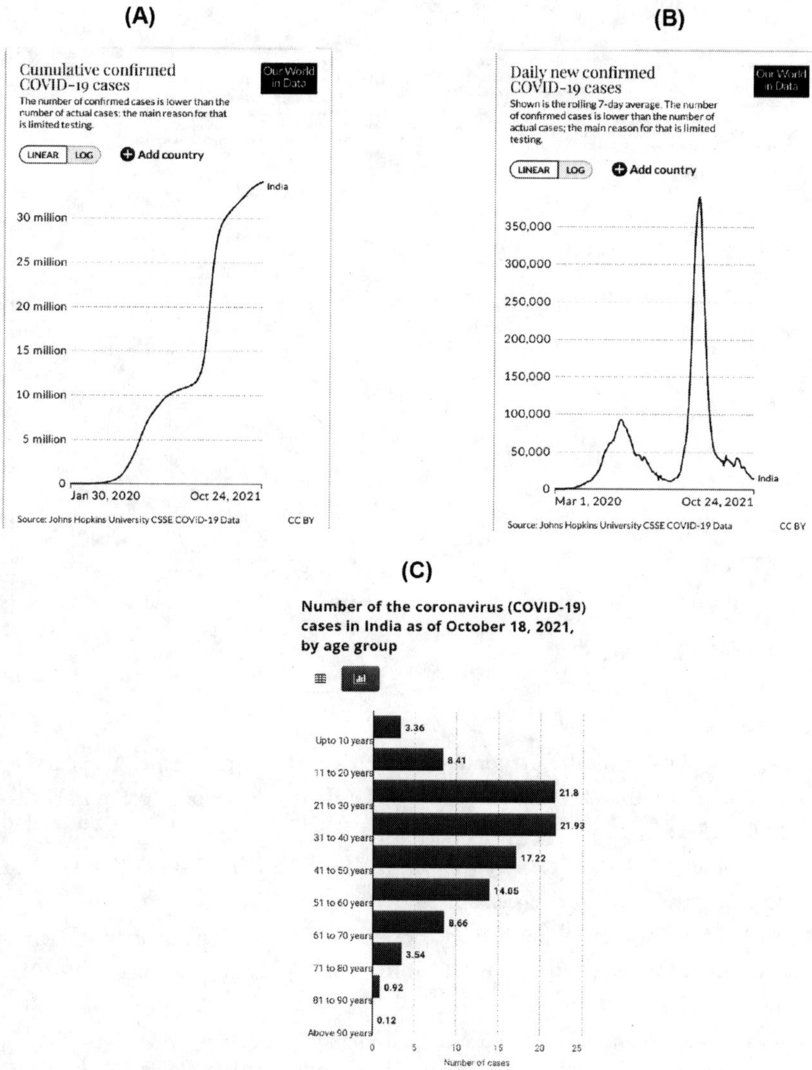

Source: Our World in Data and Statista.

Figure 30. COVID-19-releted deaths in India: **(A)** Cumulative confirmed COVID-19 deaths as of October 24, 2021 **(B)** Daily new confirmed COVID-19 deaths as of October 24, 2021.

(A) (B)

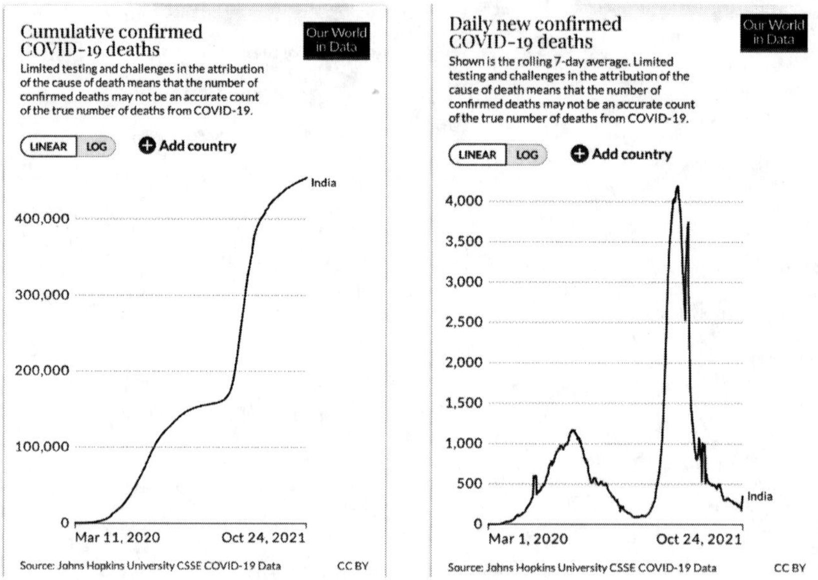

Source: Our World in Data.

References

Social capital and public health: responding to the COVID-19 pandemic. A. S.Y. Wong and J. C. Kohler. *Global Health* 16, 88 (2020). DOI: https://doi.org/10.1186/s12992-020-00615-x).

Hybrid immunity. . S. Crotty. *Science*, Vol.372, Issue 6459, pp. 1392-1393 (2021). DOI: https://doi.org/10.1126/science.abj2258

SARS-CoV-2 vaccines for all but a single dose for COVID-19 survivors. M Frieman et al. *EBioMedicine.* 2021 Jun: 68: 103401. DOI: https://doi.org/10.1016/j.ebiom.2021.103401.

mRNA vaccinations boosts cross-variant neutralizing antibodies elicited by SARS-CoV-2 infection. L. Stamatatos et al., *Science.* 2021 Mar 25; eabg9175. DOI: https://doi.org/10.1126/science.abg9175.

Prior SARS-CoV-2 infection rescues B and T cell responses to variants after first vaccine dose. C.J. Reynolds et al., *Science.* 2021 Apr 30; eabh1282. DOI: https://doi.org/10.1126/science.abh1282.

Attributes and predictors of long COVID. C. H. Sudre et al. *Nat Med* 27, 626-631 (2021). DOI: https://doi.org/10.1038/s41591-021-01292-y

https://www.who.int/india.news/feature-stories/detail/india-rolls-out-the-world-s-largest-covid-19-vaccination-drive

Strategy for COVID-19 vaccination in India: the country with the second highest population and number of cases. M.K. Velayudhan et al. *NPJ Vaccines.* 2021 April 21; 6(1): 60. DOI: https://doi.org/10.1038/s41541-021-00327-2.

World's largest vaccination drive in India: Challenges and recommendations.

G. Vaghela et al. *Health Sci Rep.* 2021 Sep; 4(3): e355. DOI: https://doi.org/10.1002/hsr2.355.

Story of the biggest vaccination drive in the world so far. M. Sharma. *Journal of Pharmacovigilance and Drug Research.* Vol. 2 No. 2 (2021): April-June 2021.

India's COVID-19 vaccination drive: key challenges and resolutions. O. P. Choudhary et al. *Lancet Infect Dis.* 2021 September 13. DOI: https://doi.org/10.1016/S1473-3099(21)00567-3.

COVID-19 vaccination drive in India-Beginning of the end. R. Bansal and P. Bansal. *J Family Med Prim Care.* 2021 July; 10(7): 2726-2727. DOI: https://doi.org/10.4103/jfmpc_294_21.

The COVID-19 Vaccination Drive: A Global Update

"This is what I call corrected science. You'll learn, you implement, you study it, and we're trying to make it better...And that's what we're catching up now-the idea of how we can provide even better protection [with additional COVID vaccine doses]."

– MPR, Oct 18, 2021

"Science appears calm and triumphant when it is completed; but science in the process of being done is only contradiction and torment, hope and disappointment."

– Pierre Paul Emile Roux

"Every person vaccinated is helping to save lives, and give us back those moments that we've missed so much."

– Global Citizen Impact

Since the beginning of 2021, the biggest vaccination campaign in history has been undertaken worldwide. As of September 2021, about 43.5 per cent of the world population has received at least one dose of a COVID-19 vaccine. 5.98 billion doses have been administered worldwide, and 28.8 million are now administered each day. However, only 2 per cent of people in low-income countries have received at least one dose.

Furthermore, the vaccination data encompasses April 04, 2021 to July 07, 2021, that includes Delta COVID-19 strain, that is more resistance to vaccinations, dominance started June 20, 2021 in 13 US jurisdictions, such as Alabama (AL), Arizona (AZ), Colorado (CO),

Indiana (IN), Los Angeles (LA) country and LA, Maryland (MD), Minnesota (MN), New Mexico (NM), New York City (NYC), Seattle, and Utah (UT). Total number of COVID-19 infections among the unvaccinated population, during this period was 569,142 (92%) and for the vaccinated people 46,312 (8%). The hospitalization rates were 34,972 (92%) and 2,976 (8%) for unvaccinated and vaccinated people respectively. Moreover, the number of deaths was 6,132 (91%) and 616 (9%) for unvaccinated and vaccinated people respectively. The data clearly shows the effectiveness of vaccines in mitigating the severity of COVID-19 disease in individuals that includes, most lethal Delta strain of COVID-19.

Additionally, the vaccination data from Israel on severe case of COVID-19, further suggest the real-world effectiveness of the COVID-19 vaccine. In this study, 17 per cent of unvaccinated population accounts for 65 per cent of all serious COVID-19 cases. Among 664 severely ill, 437 were completely unvaccinated, 168 received 2 doses, and 59 had received booster vaccination. On a per capita basis, for every serious case in higher than 60 years of individuals that received booster, there were 33 cases or unvaccinated individuals who were above 60 years of old. Additionally, for every dead higher than 60 that received booster, there were 15 deaths among unvaccinated individuals.

Moreover, as natural immunity builds in the population against COVID-19 disease, SARS-CoV-2 variants may be increasingly selected as immune escape variants. Thus, it would be interesting to know the real-world effectiveness of vaccines, in managing the different variants of COVID-19 in the population. Interestingly, vaccination, even when partial, is unlikely to contribute significantly to the emergence of escape variants, due to vaccines' ability to strongly restrict the evolutionary, and antigenic escape pathways, that give SARS-CoV-2 competitive advantages, to produce more such COVID-19 variants.

In addition, head to head comparison among three vaccines, such as Moderna, Pfizer-BioNtech, and Johnson & Johnson, higher vaccine effectiveness was observed for Moderna vaccine in comparison with two other vaccines. Also, Johnson & Johnson single-shot COVID-19 vaccine showed strong and long-lasting protection in the real world. The largest real-world evidence study for a COVID-19 vaccine reported to date, in the USA, demonstrated vaccine effectiveness of 79 per cent (CI, 77%-80%) for COVID-19-related infections, and 81 per cent (CI, 79%-84%) for COVID-19-related hospitalizations. There was no indication of reduced vaccine effectiveness during the study period, including when Delta variant became dominant in the USA. However, sequencing data were not available for more detailed analysis. The study included 390,000 people, who received the Johnson & Johnson vaccine, versus about 1.52 million unvaccinated people, matched on age, sex, time, three-digit zip code, and comorbidities, and predictors for COVID-19 infection severity conducted from March to Late July 2021. These data were consistent with the Phase 3 clinical trial vaccine efficacy results.

Lately, Moderna Phase III extended trial data, on its mRNA vaccine, has been released in a peer-reviewed publication. The trial clearly shows safety and persistent efficacy of the vaccine over 5 months period. The original publication documented results to 64 days of follow up. The extended results did not find any major safety issues, such as, anaphylaxis (2 cases), Bell's palsy (3 in placebo, 8 in vaccinated group), myocarditis (none in either cohort) and pericarditis (2 cases each in placebo and vaccinated group). Moreover, robust protection from severe illness, death, and asymptomatic infection was found.

Efficacy was observed among various subgroups, as well. Importantly, hospitalization of unvaccinated individuals cost more treatment cost, due to longer duration of the hospital stay, and the complexities of the disease prognosis in the victims.

In science, without data, we are just opinionated people. Additionally, it is important that data are supported by solid mechanistic evidence. A new study showed that a low dose (100 μg) mRNA vaccine was capable of inducing a potent humoral response, and T-lymphocytes-mediated immunity, in the vaccinated individuals. Also, potency of the neutralizing antibodies, from vaccinated individual, collected at several time points after vaccination, was measured *in vitro* experiments, in terms of pseudovirus neutralization, and live virus neutralization, against various variants of SARS-CoV-2, ACE2 receptor competition, RBD binding, and their spike binding abilities. The data reveals the underlying mechanisms of the efficacy of the neutralizing antibodies, collected from vaccinated individuals, in combating COVID-19 variants.

Furthermore, another evidence of COVID-19 vaccines' effectiveness has come from initial results on childhood vaccinations. Pfizer-BioNTech announced results (September 20, 2021), from a COVID-19 vaccine Phase 2/3 trial, showing a favorable safety profile, and robust neutralizing antibody responses, in children between 5 and 11 years of old, using a two-dose regimen of 10 μg administered 21 days apart, a smaller dose than the 30 μg dose used for people 12 and older (September 20, 2021). Moreover, results in children under 5 years of age are expected, as soon as later this year.

Taken together, while more research is still needed, early studies suggest an efficacy of higher than 70 per cent is needed, to eliminate the COVID-19 infection in the population. However, a prophylactic vaccine, with an efficacy less than 70 per cent, will be still useful, and can significantly reduce the duration of infections in infected individuals.

Another concern is the phenomenon known as ADE (Antibody Dependent Enhancement) of COVID-19 disease, and it should be taken into major consideration in developing vaccines against SARS-CoV-2. ADE has been previously observed with other coronaviruses, such as MERS-CoV and SARS-CoV. ADE happens when antibodies bind to the virus, but, instead of neutralizing the virus, the resulting antibody-virus complex facilitates viral entry by host macrophages. In addition, inactivated vaccines pose a risk, as they can cause VAERD (Vaccine-associated enhanced respiratory disease), observed in the past, with measles and RSV in humans. Additionally, pre-existing immunity to adenoviruses is also a major concern, especially for those vaccine candidates, that use human adenovirus as vector, as it may result in a reduced response to the vaccines.

Finally, as with any new inventions, there are scopes of improvement that are typically figured out in trial and tested approach. In spite of limitations, it is becoming increasingly evident that vaccines are effective in reducing the transmission of COVID-19 infections, hospitalization, fatality of the disease, and mortality rates, around the world, that in turn significantly reduces the economic burden on the global society.

Figure 31. Global vaccination drive: **(A)** Per cent share of people in different countries who are either partially or fully vaccinated as of September 20, 2021 **(B)** Number of vaccine doses administered per 100 people around the world **(C)** Number of vaccine doses administered per 100 people by continent.

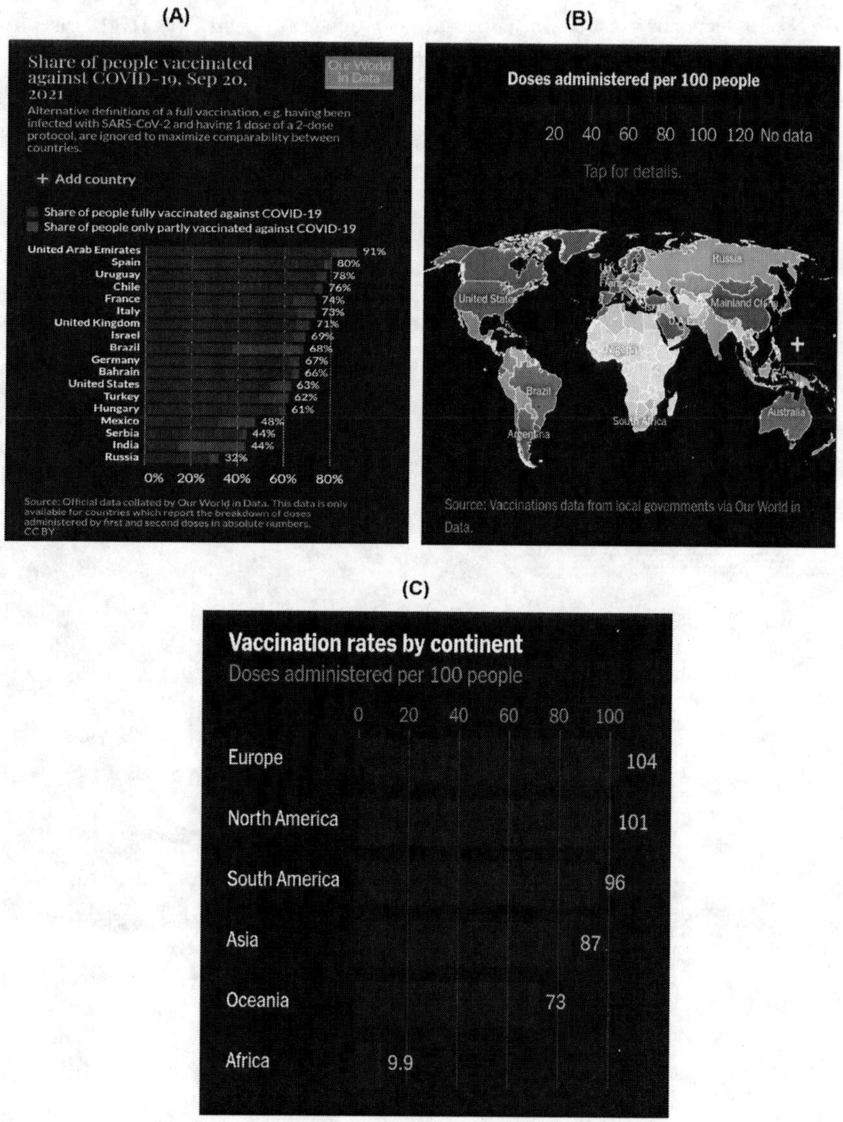

Source: Our World in Data.

Figure 32. Measurement of real-world effectiveness of mRNA vaccines between April 04 and September 04, 2021 in the U.S. **(A),** numbers, percentage, and incidence rate ratios in fully vaccinated and unvaccinated COVID-19 patients including hospitalizations, and deaths by age group across 13 U.S jurisdictions, April 4-June 19 and June 20-July 17, 2021 **(B),** rate of COVID-19 cases by vaccination status and age group **(C),** rate of COVID-19 deaths by vaccination status and age group **(D),** rate of COVID-19 cases or deaths by vaccination status and vaccine product.

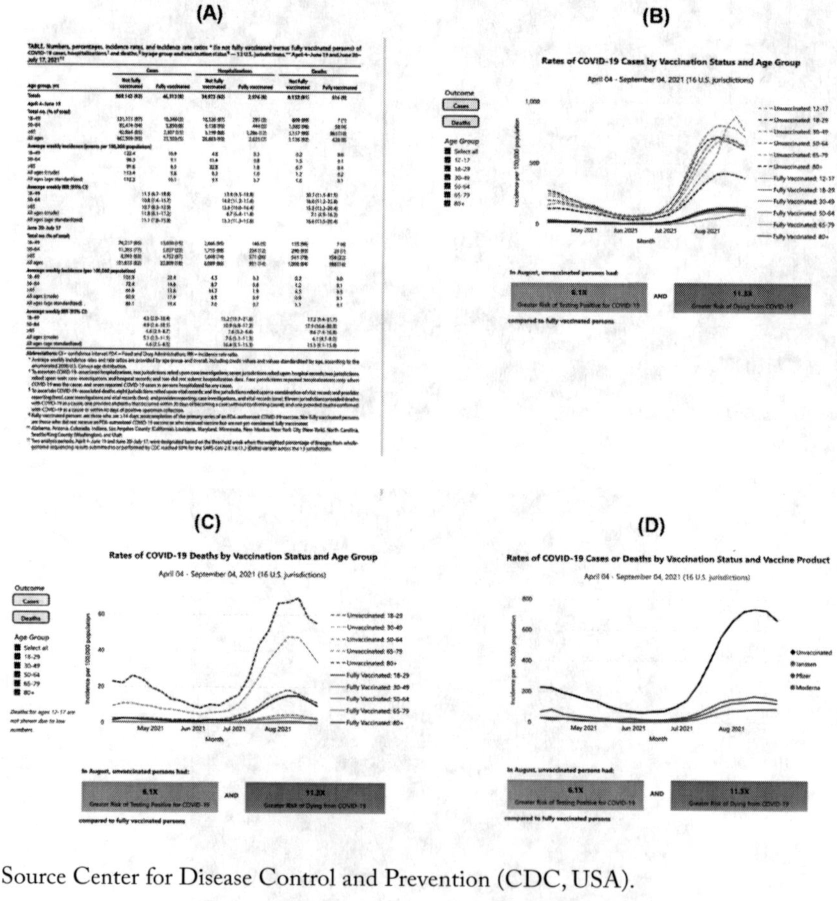

Source Center for Disease Control and Prevention (CDC, USA).

Figure 33. Israel's serious COVID-19 cases by vaccination status-unvaccinated, vaccinated with two doses of vaccine, and vaccinated with additional booster vaccine dose.

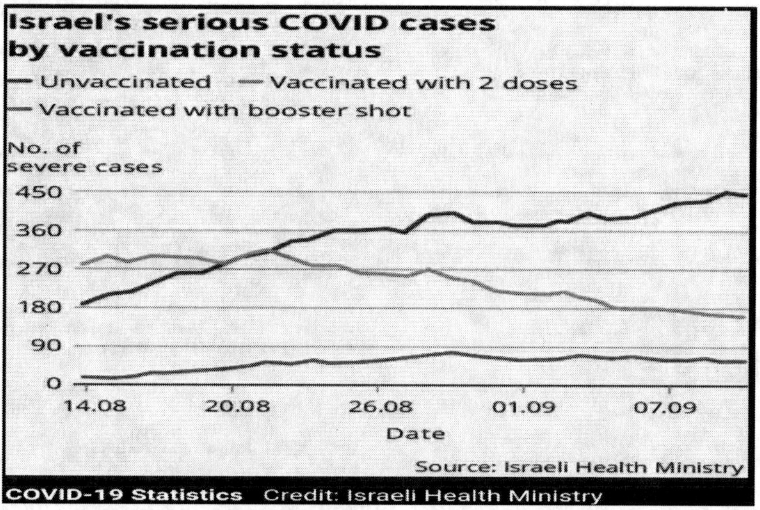

Source: COVID-19 Statistics, Israeli Health Ministry.

Figure 34. (A) Real-world effectiveness in percentage of Pfizer-BioNTech, Oxford, Moderna, J&J, Noravax, and Sinovac vaccines by COVID-19 variant types (alpha and delta). **(B),** comparison of vaccines' effectiveness among Moderna, Pfizer-BioNTech, and Johnson & Johnson by COVID-19 hospitalization rates.

(A)

Table 1. Vaccine effectiveness in % (95% CI) or mean

Outcome	Alpha	Delta	Beta/Gamma
Symptomatic infection			
Pfizer-BioNTech	90 (85–95)	85 (80–90)	85 (70–93)
Oxford	80 (70–85)	70 (60–75)	<70 [–76.8–54.8] (mild COVID-19 only)[b]
Moderna	91 (84, 95)	70 (45–85)	78 (60–88) [1 dose]
J&J	N/A	N/A	52 (30.3–67.4)
Novavax	86	60	60
Sinovac	N/A	N/A	65.9 (65.2–66.6)?
Severe disease			
Pfizer-BioNTech	95 (90–99)	95 (90–99)	98 (82–100)
Oxford	95 (80–99)	95 (80–99)	N/A
Moderna	94 (90, 97)	96 (72–99) [1 dose]	94 (75–99) [1 dose]
J&J	N/A	71	65–66 (hospitalization) 91–95 (mortality)
Sinovac	N/A	N/A	87.5 (86.7–88.2)
Infection			
Pfizer-BioNTech	Variable[a]	Variable[a]	Variable[a]
Oxford	55–80	50–87	70–79 (limited data)
Moderna			

[a]Vaccine effectiveness against infection is a dynamic figure that varies by setting, testing criteria, behavior, community prevalence, exposure risk, immunity status, and time from vaccination.
[b]Please see the text for detailed explanation of this study.

(B)

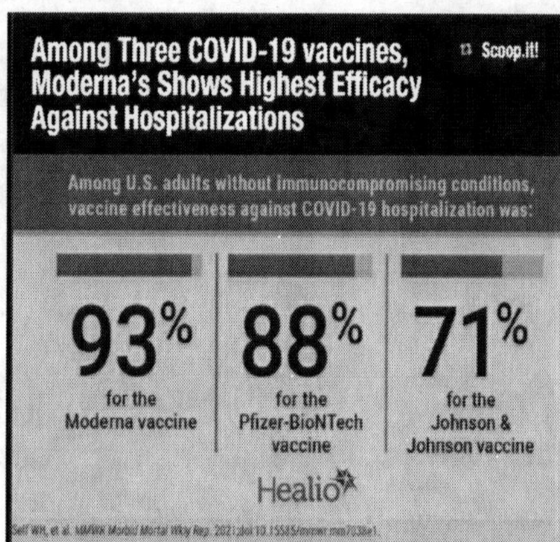

Source: *Nature* 2021 and *MMWR Morbid Mortal Wkly Rep* 2021.

Figure 35. (A) Comparison of deaths between vaccinated and unvaccinated population in the period June-September 2021 and **(B),** economic burden of treatment in hospitalized COVID-19 patients who are unvaccinated.

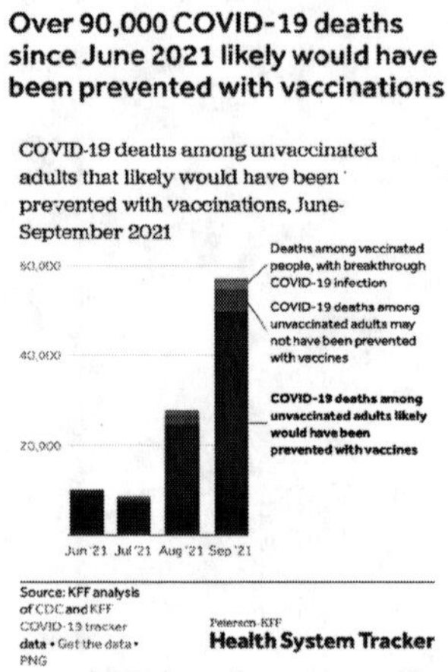

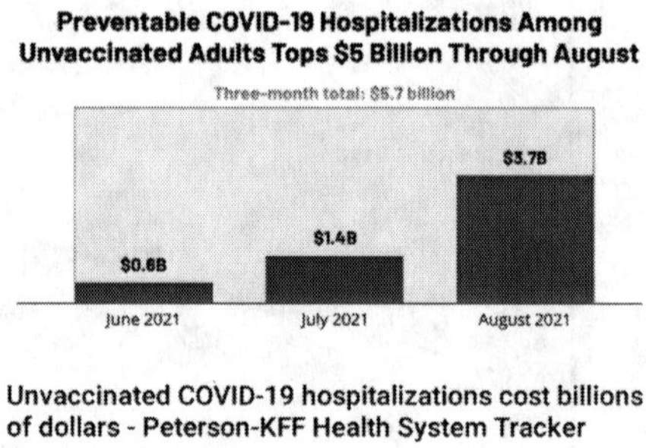

Source: KFF analysis of CDC and KFF COVID-19 tracker data and Peterson-KFF Health System Tracker.

Figure 36. Assessment of myocarditis after COVID-19 vaccination (BNT162b2 mRNA (Pfizer-BioNTech)) among health care personnel in Israel.

Population	Total Study Population	All Cases of Myocarditis		Fulminant Myocarditis		Intermediate Myocarditis		Mild Myocarditis	
		No. of Cases	Cumulative Incidence (95% CI)	No. of Cases	Cumulative Incidence (95% CI)	No. of Cases	Cumulative Incidence (95% CI)	No. of Cases	Cumulative Incidence (95% CI)
	no.		*no./100,000 persons*		*no./100,000 persons*		*no./100,000 persons*		*no./100,000 persons*
All vaccinated patients	2,558,421	54	2.13 (1.56–2.70)	1	0.04 (0–0.12)	12	0.47 (0.21–0.74)	41	1.62 (1.12–2.11)
Male sex	1,248,433	51	4.12 (2.99–5.26)	1	0.08 (0–0.24)	11	0.89 (0.36–1.42)	39	3.15 (2.16–4.14)
Female sex	1,309,988	3	0.23 (0–0.49)	0	0	1	0.08 (0–0.23)	2	0.15 (0–0.37)
Sex and age group									
Either sex, 16–29 yr	593,648	32	5.49 (3.59–7.39)	1	0.17 (0–0.50)	6	1.03 (0.21–1.85)	25	4.29 (2.61–5.97)
Either sex, ≥30 yr	1,964,773	22	1.13 (0.66–1.60)	0	0	6	0.31 (0.06–0.56)	16	0.82 (0.42–1.22)
Male sex, 16–29 yr	295,288	31	10.69 (6.93–14.46)	1	0.34 (0–1.01)	6	2.06 (0.41–3.72)	24	8.29 (4.97–11.61)
Male sex, ≥30 yr	953,145	20	2.11 (1.19–3.04)	0	0	5	0.53 (0.07–0.99)	15	1.58 (0.78–2.38)
Female sex, 16–29 yr	298,360	1	0.34 (0–1)	0	0	0	0	1	0.34 (0–1)
Female sex, ≥30 yr	1,011,628	2	0.20 (0–0.48)	0	0	1	0.10 (0–0.30)	1	0.10 (0–0.29)

* The cumulative incidence per 100,000 persons was estimated with the use of the Kaplan–Meier method.

Source: G. Witberg et al. *New England Journal of Medicine*, 2021.

Figure 37. Response to low-dose mRNA-1273 vaccination over 7 months: **(A-B)** Immunological memory of antibodies, CD4+ T cells, and CD8+ T cells was examined after low-dose mRNA vaccination. Levels of spike-specific immune memory were then compared to immune memory observed after natural infection with SARS-CoV-2 or after full-dose vaccination. Robust immune memory **(A)** comparable to natural infection but lower than full-dose vaccination was observed. Increased vaccine age correlated with reduced antibody levels **(B)** but had no effect on cellular immune memory **(A)** Immune memory was enhanced by preexisting cross-reactive T cells. D1: day 1.

(A)

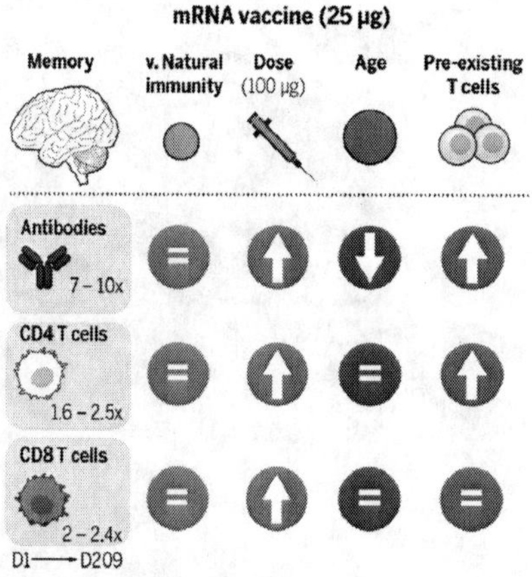

Immunological memory of antibodies, CD4⁺ T cells, and CD8 T cells was examined after a low dose of mRNA vaccination.

(B)

Assay	Variant	% of sera with detectable antibodies			
		Day 29	Day 43	Day 119	Day 209
Pseudovirus Neutralization	WA1	25%	100%	100%	88%
	D614G	83%	100%	100%	100%
	B.1.1.7	33%	100%	100%	96%
	B.1.351	8%	100%	71%	54%
	P.1	*not tested*	100%	*not tested*	85%
	B.1.429	*not tested*	100%	*not tested*	100%
	B.1.526	*not tested*	100%	*not tested*	88%
	B.1.617.2	*not tested*	100%	*not tested*	96%
Live-Virus Neutralization	WA1	79%	100%	100%	100%
	D614G	67%	100%	100%	100%
	B.1.1.7	54%	100%	100%	88%
	B.1.351	8%	100%	79%	58%
ACE2 Competition	WA1	100%	100%	100%	100%
	B.1.1.7	83%	100%	100%	100%
	B.1.351	63%	100%	71%	79%
Cell-Surface Spike Binding	WA1	100%	100%	100%	100%
	D614G	100%	100%	100%	100%
	B.1.1.7	100%	100%	100%	100%
	B.1.351	100%	100%	100%	100%
	P.1	100%	100%	100%	100%
	B.1.429	100%	100%	100%	100%
	B.1.526	100%	100%	100%	100%
	B.1.617.2	100%	100%	100%	100%
S-2P Binding	WA1	100%	100%	100%	100%
	B.1.1.7	100%	100%	100%	100%
	B.1.351	100%	100%	100%	100%
	P.1	100%	100%	100%	100%
RBD Binding	WA1	100%	100%	100%	100%
	B.1.1.7	100%	100%	100%	100%
	B.1.351	100%	100%	100%	100%
	P.1	100%	100%	100%	100%

0% — 100%

Source: J. Mateus *Science* 14 Sep 2021.

Figure 38. Parenteral vaccine-mediated immunity and possible mechanisms of transmission reduction. (A) Intramuscular immunization of currently approved COVID-19 vaccines elicits systemic IgG and IgA responses. In some cases, dimeric IgA can be transported across the mucosal epithelia. Some of the serum antibodies are transported or spill over into the respiratory mucosa to prevent viral entry into host airway epithelial cells. (B) Intra-host replication and viral spread can be prevented by the IgG and IgA antibodies along with T cells specific to the virus. (C) If the vaccines reduce symptoms such as coughing and sneezing, the emission load from the vaccinated individuals will be reduced, leading to less effective transmission of virus to others. (D) If virus manages to replicate within the respiratory mucosa, vaccine-induced immune responses will reduce transmittable viral load within the upper respiratory tract (UTR) and lower respiratory tract (LTR). Furthermore, antibodies might cause virus less infectious in the recipient host, preventing subsequent inter-host transmission.

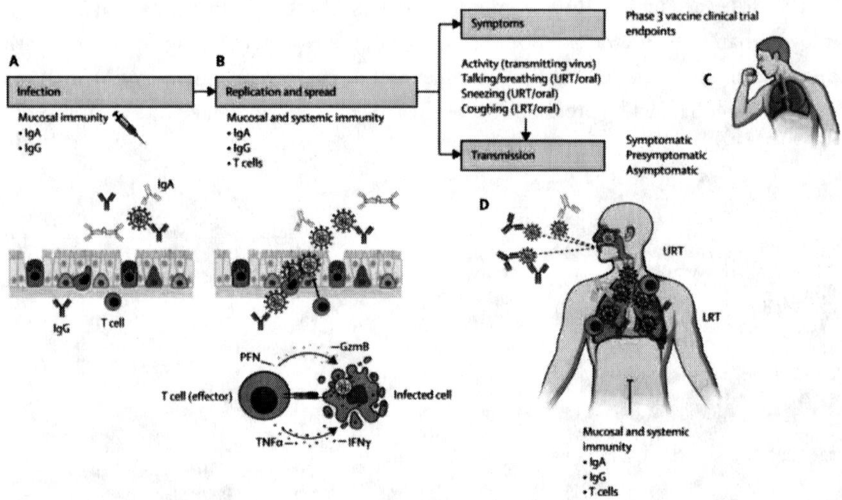

Source: *Lancet Infectious Disease*, 2021.

References

https://wwwhaaretz.com.cdn.ampproject.org/c/s/www.haaretz.com/amp/israel-news/israel-unvaccinated-booster-65-serious-covid-19-cases-death-delta-1.10208784

Memory B cell repertoire for recognition of evolving SARS-CoV-2. P. Tong et al. *Cell* Vol. 184, Issue 19, 16 September 2021, Pages 4969-4980.e15. DOI: https://doi.org/10.1016/j.cell.2021.07.025

New Data Confirms Strong and Long-Lasting Protection of Johnson & Johnson COVID-19 Vaccine. www.jnj.com

Efficacy of the mRNA-1273 SARS-CoV-2 vaccine at completion of blinded phase. M. Hana et al. *The New England Journal of Medicine*, September 22, 2021. DOI: https://doi.org/10.1056/NEJMoa2113017.

Does infection with or vaccination against SARS-CoV-2 lead to lasting immunity? G. Milne et al. *The Lancet* October 21, 2021. DOI: https://doi.org/10.1016/S2213-2600(21)00407-0.

https://www.businesswire.com/news/home/20210920005452/en.

Pfizer COVID vaccine protects against worrying coronavirus variants. E. Callaway. *Nature* 593, 325-326 (2021). DOI: https://doi.org/10.1038/d41586-021-01222-5.

Safety and efficacy of the ChAdOx1 nCoV-19 vaccine (AZD 1222) against SARS-CoV-2: an interim analysis of four randomised controlled trials in Brazil, South Africa, and the UK. M. Voysey et al. *The Lancet.* Vol. 397, Issue 10269, P99-111, January 09, 2021. DOI: https://doi.org/10.1016/S0140-6736(20)32661-1.

Effectiveness of Covvid-19 vaccines against the B.1.617.2 (Delta) variant. J. L. Bernal et al. *The New England Journal of Medicine* 2021; 385:585-594. DOI: https://doi.org/10.1056/NEJMoa2108891.

Low-dose mRNA-1273 COVID-19 vaccine generates durable memory enhanced by cross-reactive T cells. J. Mateus et al. *Science* Vol. 374, No. 6566, 14 September 2021. DOI: https://doi.org/10.1126/science.abj9853.

Making sense of mutations: what D614G means for the COVID-19 pandemic remains unclear. N. D. Grubaugh et al. *Cell.* (2020) 182:794-5. DOI: https://doi.org/10.1016/j.cell.2020.06.040).

The improbability of the rapid development of a vaccine for SARS-CoV-2. K.V. Morris. *Mol Ther.* (2020) 28:1548-49. DOI: https://doi.org/10.1016/j.ymthe.2020.06.005.

Rapid COVID-19 vaccine development. B.S. Graham et al. *Science.* (2020) 368: 945-6. DOI: https://doi.org/10.1126/science.abb8923).

Immunogenicity and safety of a recombinant adenovirus type-5-vectored COVID-19 vaccine in healthy adults aged 18 years or older: a randomized, double blind, placebo-controlled, phase 2 trial. Zhu FC et al. *Lancet.* (2020) 396:479-88. DOI: https://doi.org/10.1016/S0140-6736(20)31605-6.

Myocarditis after Covid-19 Vaccination in a Large Health Care Organization. G. Witberg et al. *The New England Journal of Medicine,* October 6, 2021. DOI: https://doi.org/10.1056/NEJMoa2110737.

PART TWO

The Multifaceted Societal Impact of COVID-19 on Science & Technology, and Innovation: Indian and Global Perspective

Towards a Better Normal: An Indian Perspective

> "We are today living in a Covid world. Every sphere of our public and personal life has changed and will change further. We are all in it together; the virus does not respect boundaries of any kind. We are asking for a rethink. We must create a better normal."
>
> – India Today, October 25, 2021.

> "The greatest lesson this pandemic has taught everyone, even the sceptics, is that scientific discovery is the crucial to human flourishing."
>
> – Kiran Mazumdar Shaw

> "As the world moves from a BC to AD reality….before coronavirus to after disease….we have arrived at the dawn of the age of digital learning."
>
> – Deborah Quazzo. GSV Ventures

Since the beginning of the ongoing pandemic, India stood firm to manage the unprecedented crisis, caused by the COVID-19 pandemic, with strong supports from both government, and non-government organizations, accelerating diagnostic and research infrastructures, preventive, and therapeutic healthcare facilities, to save the lives of Indian citizens.

However, second wave of pandemic, has caused a major havoc in the Indian society, in part, due to its rapidity, and intensity over a short period of time. Despite this difficulty, as of now, the mortality rate in the Indian population is substantially lower compared to advanced nations, such as the USA and UK in spite of comparatively much lower rate of full-vaccination (30%), indicating a strong performance of the Indian healthcare system, in mitigating the loss of lives, through effective treatment of the hospitalized COVID-19 patients. This is indeed appreciable, as LMICs do not always have the financial luxury of complete lockdown for long period of time.

Moreover, as the saying goes 'blessings often come in disguise', the COVID-19 pandemic 2020, brought noticeable attention on STI (Science & Technology, Innovation (STI)), with key focus on health sciences. Not only the public health, but, also the fundamental mechanism(s) of COVID-19 disease transmission, and new scientific information, that help to mitigate the deadly disease, become part of mainstream discussions, that includes less science-conscious people, who became aware of pressing issues, such as complexities of vaccine development, and the updated knowledge about the progression of clinical trails in vaccine, and non-vaccine pharmacological interventions.

Additionally, the renaissance knowledge about India's inherent scientific capabilities, vaccine development, and its large-scale manufacturing, trending biotechnology, and information technology startup culture, powerful national and international scientific and industrial collaborations, a redefined healthcare system, together with innovative science policy, at the time of pandemic, will only help the Indian society, in the long run, to develop an enriched scientific and innovative mindset, that will further help to foster and appreciate more new innovations, and their subsequent wider adoptions, as the responsible, and progressive citizens of the country. Thus, convergence of science and society during the COVID-19 pandemic, is one of the most significant accomplishments, the Indian civilization has ever achieved.

In order to showcase the impressive progress in STI, in the early phase of COVID-19 pandemic, to promote scientific awareness in the society, 'Vigyan Prasar', an autonomous organization of the Department of Science & Technology (DST), Government of India, published a first updated report on April 18, 2020. Subsequently, more such reports periodically released by 'Vigyan Prasar'. The document "Science and Technology Efforts on COVID-19 in India" serves as a useful guide, for policy makers, scientists, research scholars, and other stakeholders, who might be interested in understanding, and keep themselves updated with the latest STI efforts being made, to develop effective solutions to COVID-19-related problems.

Furthermore, to establish a useful STI policy, a core strategy group (CSG) has been set up, in Council of Scientific and Industrial Research (CSIR), Government of India, and five verticals have been identified, under which COVID-19-related activities are being carried out. These include: Digital & Molecular Surveillance; Rapid and Cost-effective Diagnostics; New Drugs/Repurposing of Drugs and Accessories; Hospital Assistive Devices and Personal Protective Kits (PPEs); and Supply Chain and Logistics Support. CSIR labs nationwide have begun testing swab samples of COVID-19 patients, and some of the CSIR institutes across the nation, such as Centre for Cellular and Molecular Biology (CCMB-CSIR), Hyderabad, have started doing the genetic sequencing of the COVID-19 virus, and their emerging variants. Also, Sree Chitra Tirnual Institute for Medical Sciences and Technology, Thiruvanathapuram, an institute of national importance of DST, has developed a diagnostic kit, that can confirm COVID-19 in 2 hours at low cost (Science and Technology Efforts on COVID-19 in India, Vigyan Prasar, 2020). The test that detects the N gene of SARS-CoV-2, using reverse transcriptase (RT) loop-mediated amplification of viral nucleic acid (RT-LAMP), is one of the world's new detection tests for COVID-19. They have also developed the innovative specific RNA extraction kit that goes with RT-LAMP. The technology has been transferred to a private company, for large-scale manufacturing, that has operations in many countries, highlighting the importance of public-private collaboration, at the time of crisis.

In addition to CSIR and DST, Government of India; Department of Biotechnology (DBT), Indian Council of Medical Research (ICMR), Ministry of Health & Family Welfare, Defense Research and Development Organization (DRDO), Ministry of Electronics and Information Technology (MeitY), and other Scientific and Academic Institutions, and Private Sector Enterprises have been playing key roles in strengthening the collective S&T and innovation efforts of India. Importantly, the Office of Principal Scientific Advisor (PSA), Government of India, has developed a "Handbook for COVID-19 testing in Research Institutions", that allows many labs follow an uniform preparedness, in terms of equipments, staffs and expertise needed for COVID-19 testing.

Moreover, new developments on the mitigation of COVID-19 periodically published for the general public, by the Government of India. For example, in the recent update (COVID-19: Science & Technology Efforts in India, Vol. IV, Issue 8, August 2021), a major collaborative effort, where scientists from India, Russia, Brazil, and South Africa will work together to repurpose, validate, and synthesize lead compounds, against main protease and RNA replicase; the enzyme that catalyzes the replication of RNA of SARS-CoV-2, has been discussed. This approach can potentially produce new medicine that could inhibit the maturation, and propagation of SARS-CoV-2, inside human cells, reducing viral load inside the body. In addition, COVID-19 analytics portal has been developed by the ICMR. Various private and government labs that are testing COVID-19 samples will upload the data on the portal that also includes all information about the COVID-19 patients. The data will be primarily used by Union Ministry of Health and Family Welfare (MoHFW) to formulate testing strategy for each individual state.

Additionally, Indian Institute of Science (IISc), Bangalore, has developed an Artificial Intelligence (AI) tool (CoviHawkes) that can forecast and monitor COVID-19 infections across the country. CoviHawkes can help policymakers identify key regions that need lockdown to control the spread of COVID-19 infection. Such, localized lockdowns would offer a better alternative to statewide or nationwide lockdowns. The tool has the ability to combine the observed patterns in the previous case counts with additional factors, such as demographics (population density) and mobility (decrease or increase in the percentage of people travelling for work) of the region. Also, the ICMR has developed COVID-19 sample collection management system for rapid antigen, antibody, and RT-PCR tests. This will help government to disseminate the key information throughout the country. Importantly, India's first indigenous, cost-effective, wireless physiological monitoring system for COVID-19 patients, COVID BEEP, has been developed by ESIC medical College Hyderabad in collaboration with Electronics Corporation of India Ltd. (ECIL) and the Department of Atomic Energy (DAE). COVID BEEP can measure body temperature, blood oxygen saturation, heart rate, respiratory rate, ECG, blood pressure, and location of the patient.

Following a rich tradition of Indian Ayurveda, the ministry of AYUSH (Ayurveda, Yoga & Naturopathy, Unani, Siddha and Homeopathy) has formed an inter-disciplinary AYUSH R&D task force with the help of CSIR, ICMR, DBT, All India Institute of Medical Sciences (AIIMS), and AYUSH Institutions. The task force has formulated and designed clinical research protocols for prophylactic studies and add-on interventions in COVID-19 victims for studying four different interventions such as Ashwagandha, Yashtimadhu, Guduchi and Pippali, and a poly-herbal formulation (AYUSH-64). Through robust clinical trials conducted by the CSIR and Central Council for Research in Ayurvedic Sciences (CCRAS), AYUSH-64, has been scientifically validated for its usefulness in the treatment of asymptomatic and mild COVID-19 cases as an adjunct to standard care.

Moreover, scientists from BRICS (India, China, Brazil, Russia, South Africa) countries, in collaboration with DST, is carrying out genomic sequencing of SARS-CoV-2 and studies on the epidemiology, and mathematical modeling of COVID-19 pandemic in India. This will significantly boost the efforts in detecting genetic mutations, by high-throughput genomic surveillance, and new COVID-19 variants, as well as distribution of the virus in the population, and also can make projections about the future of its spread.

Another important milestone in India's STI effort is the development of heat-tolerant vaccine against COVID-19 viral variants, developed by IISc., Bangalore. The vaccine works well against all key COVID-19 variants of concern: Alpha, Beta, Gamma, and Delta. The vaccine is stable at 37°C for a month, and can withstand transient exposure to temperature, as high as 100°C. Thus, it is useful in countries, such as India, where cold storage and transportation, especially in remote areas are expensive and challenging. One of the improved formulations is being rapidly moved to clinical development. Furthermore, the National Institute of Animal Biotechnology (NIAB) collaborates with Translational Health Science and Technology Institute (THSTI), Faridabad, to test anti-viral compounds without the need to culture coronaviruses that poses significant health risk to the researchers. The idea is to make artificial coronaviruses without the critical genetic elements, essential for virus replication. The technology platform can be used for screening multiple compounds simultaneously, against coronaviruses from past, present, and future. It is expected that it will facilitate rapid progression for identifying key compounds through preliminary screening. Also, InStem (Institute for Stem Cell Science and Regenerative Medicine), Bangalore, an autonomous institute of DBT, is currently examining if a specific class of molecules, called antimicrobial peptides (AMPs), produced in the body, is capable of combating the COVID-19 virus. These AMPs have the potential to block the initial infection as antiviral immunity, and can limit the viral load in the infected patients to reduce the severity of the disease. Importantly, this approach will serve as an additional protection, along with COVID-19 appropriate behaviors (NPIs). Also, National Institute of Biomedical Genomics (NIBMG), Kolkata, an autonomous institute of DBT, is developing a novel virus-like particle (VLP) in collaboration with IISc, Bangalore. VLP specific to the Indian strain of SARS-CoV-2 will pave the way for the development of a vaccine against the SARS-CoV-2. Moreover, Center of Innovative and Applied Bioprocessing (CIAB) is developing a series of photosensitizer nano formulations. One of the formulations exhibited very high efficacy, similar to clinically tested drug Ramdesivir, to destroy SARS-CoV-2 *in vitro*.

Human monoclonal antibodies (mAbs) have the potential to be used for both prevention and treatment of an infectious disease. Interestingly, over 200 human mAbs from single-cell sorted memory B-lymphocyte cells derived from COVID-19 recovered patients, have been generated, and analyzed for their efficacy on neutralizing SARS-CoV-2. The positive clones will be further expanded *in vitro,* and mAbs can be collected in large quantities from the culture media, and purified. Also, The International Center for Genetic Engineering and Biotechnology (ICGEB) is collaborating with NIMR (National Institute of Malaria Research)- An Unit of ICMR and Emory University, USA, on this fascinating research. Rajiv Gandhi Centre for Biotechnology (RGCB) aims to develop cell-based assays to identify inhibitors of SARS-CoV-2 entry to the cells and inhibitors of viral protease. Few others important scientific collaborations across the country includes: IIT (Indian Institute of Technology)-Indore partnered with National Centre for Cell Sciences (NCCS), Pune, for developing pseudo-typed SARS-CoV-2; NCCS partnership with IIT-Indore and Bharat Biotech International Ltd (BBIL), for human mAbs development against SARS-CoV-2; National Institute of Plant Genome Research (NIPGR) is examining the potential use of natural plant products, flavonoids, against SARS-CoV-2; National Institute of Immunology-DBT, New Delhi, is working on identification of potential anti-COVID-19 compounds that specifically target RNA dependent RNA polymerases etc. Institute of Genomics and Integrated Biology (IGIB-CSIR), New Delhi, has been able to quickly sequence the SARS-CoV-2 and is now collaborating with ICMR, National Centre for Disease Control (NCDC), and also with multinational corporations such as Intel, to study the human-virus interaction, how they are responding to different candidate drugs, and screen them for prescribing for patients.

An important breakthrough in the technological challenge has happened lately, that plays a key role in delivering the perishable biologics, such as vaccines, through effective supply chain, keeping the efficacy of the vaccines intact during the transportation. Bangalore-based Centre for Cellular and Molecular Platforms (C-CAMP)'s startup, Blackfrog technologies has the ability to make and disseminate 100 Emvolio units: a portable, battery-operated clinical-grade refrigeration system that allows transport of biological specimens, such as vaccines. This will alleviate the cold chain disruption that affects the last-mile delivery of vaccines across the country.

Importantly, the India Science, Technology and Innovation Portal (ISTI) has been developed by Vigyan Prasar (DST) to provide a single-window source of information about all data related to the Indian STI ecosystem, by aggregating data on scientific inputs and outputs, unifying stakeholders, helping efficient use of resources and opportunities ranging from school to faculty level, and showcasing India's STI achievements.

Also, a key outreach initiative is launched by India Service Channel: internet-based Over-The-Top (OTT) science TV channel. This 24/7 video platform is dedicated for STI dissemination, with a strong focus to spreading scientific awareness, in the society, supported by the National Council of Science and Technology Communication (NCSTC), DST. In addition, myGOV reaches out to Indian citizens, by inviting them to write blog posts on mass vaccination drive, across the country that is a key step in overcoming vaccine hesitancy, and other vaccine-related questions. NITI Aayog is a key vertical, run by the Government of India, that seeks to strengthen the STI in the nation, by formulating science- and technology-specific plans/programs, and policies that also promotes Digital India Mission.

In addition, science-based startups are playing critical role, bringing technologies at rapid pace, for combating the COVID-19 pandemic in the society, and helping the nation to deal with the adverse situation. Many of them brought out new technologies, repurposed their existing technologies, scaled up operations, and commercialized them with financial support from the Government of India. For example, Pune-based Mylab Discovery was the first indigenous company, who developed a real-time PCR-based molecular diagnostic kit that screens and detects samples of people who show flu-like symptoms. The kit was further developed and approved by ICMR and CDSCO (Central Drugs Standard Control Organization). With financial support from TDB (Technology Development Board)-DST, the production of kits was ramped up in a short period of time from 30,000 tests to 0.2 million tests per day. Interestingly, Mylab has emerged as unicorn during the ongoing COVID-19 crisis, exemplifying the massive growth of a startup, at the time of crisis. Nanoclean Global, a Delhi-based company, has assembled and installed semi-automatic N95 mask production machine, and started commercialization of the their products. The company has distributed 0.1 million N95 masks to the Delhi Police in their fight against COVID-19. Pune-based Thincr Technologies India, developed low-cost masks, with anti-viral agents coated on them, to prevent transmission and protect individuals from viral infections. Evobi Automations, Bangalore has developed Ultraviolet Sanitizers that is portable and distributed to various hospitals in Mumbai and Government schools across the country. A portable X-Rays machine with Digital Imaging and Battery Back-Up was developed by Iatome Electric India, a Coimbatore-based company. It can facilitate X-ray imaging in remote and rural locations with limited or no electricity. It has also developed first version of digital Chest X-Ray machine for trial in hospital setting. "SpiroPRO", a cost-effective digital handled spirometer, useful for measuring and monitoring lung capacity, diagnosing lung infection in COVID-19 infected patients, was developed by Pune-based Briota Technologies. The product comes with a Mobile App, NEHA (Nurse Educator and Health Assistant), for monitoring of lung condition, and managing ventilator support with the help of remote telemedicine facility. The company has also developed a questionnaire-based App, called 'SAVE' that has the ability to check the spread of

COVID-19 in the population. It has the video conferencing ability, and can connect patients with medium symptoms, based on the score of the App, with the doctors. Bangalore-based Cocoslabs Innovative Solutions has developed and commercialized a high-accuracy and contactless thermal analytics product for the detection of elevated body temperature. Also, it has the ability to checking facemasks and social distance compliance automatically. They are working on AI sensor with support from TDS-DST, that will monitor oxygen levels in oxygen tankers, and alert authorities well in advance in real-time and ensure enough oxygen supply during emergency.

Science policy, science diplomacy, bilateral, and multilateral cooperation have taken the center stage during the ongoing pandemic. The rapid advancements in these areas will benefit India's STI, and their sustainment. Thus, 'Science' and 'Science-Advice' became the important component in the decision making process. The increased transparency about sharing STI-based information with the people, has enhanced the confidence and trust in STI among the general population. The National Initiative for Developing and Harnessing Innovation (NIDHI) has impacted India's Innovation ecosystem, by nurturing 3,861 startups through a network of 153 incubators nationwide with the help of DST. NIDHI and its supported network of startup incubators have been playing key roles during the COVID-19 pandemic through the "Centre for Augmenting WAR with COVID-19 Health Crisis (CAWACH)" program that supports COVID-19-realted solutions and innovations. The Technology Information, Forecasting and Assessment Council (TIFAC) has been playing major role in providing recommendations for useful technology, and policy implementation to make India "ATMANIRBHAR" in the aftermath of the pandemic. Moreover, India's fifth national science and technology policy (STIP 2020), intends to incorporate key inputs from the ongoing pandemic to further strengthen the existing STIP. The policy will emphasize the need for self-reliance in India's STI, by leveraging the country's strength in R&D, workforce, demographic dividend, diversity, and data.

Finally, the significance of science diplomacy is growing at the time of COVID-19 crisis. Science diplomacy is a good way of constructively engaging multiple nations, to solve common and critical problems, by leveraging strengths of each country, through active collaboration, in terms of infrastructure, financial assets, workforce, and ideologies. Moreover, due to the growing importance of science diplomacy in the field of research, education, and practice that aims to strengthen the link between STI and international affairs, there has been tremendous interest among early career scientists, and young diplomats to engage more effectively with the science-diplomacy nexus across the world. However, a structured basic course, addressing the commonalities of all STI issues, with a focus on international affairs is still lacking, thereby, necessitating its inclusion into the key curriculum in the educational institutions. Over many years, scientists and diplomats have been separated from each other in addressing jointly the key STI global issues beneficial to the society. COVID-19 worldwide pandemic helps them to realize the importance to working together on public health issues. A key question is can we strengthen Indian STI industry ecosystem post-pandemic using science diplomacy as a tool? Is this synonymous to business diplomacy? Thus, essentially, the COVID-19 pandemic has changed how we understand, and approach problems in STI in contemporary society.

In summary, the COVID-19 pandemic has brought STI and scientists, entrepreneurs, policy makers, and other stakeholders to the forefront of public engagements, and scrutiny. A stellar performance in managing public health issues is the key to win trust in the society.

Also, collaboration has become the essential ingredient to be successful in the fight against a deadly virus. Over many years, India has produced diverse range of scientists, whose research area offers bench expertise, directly related to the biology of the virus and its host. Thus, active collaborations among biologists from many domains of life sciences will strengthen the collective effort to effectively managing the ongoing pandemic. Moreover, theoretical physicists, statisticians, computer scientists, mathematicians, and ecologists are valuable to developing models for tracking, and predicting the outcome of infection transmission. Importantly, the social scientists, investigating the socio-behavioral factors, among diverse groups of people, that often cause transmission of infectious disease with variable impact in different sections of the society, are critical component of the collective efforts with other collaborating partners. Thus, it is time for India's public policymakers to make sure necessary data are collected, and available freely to a wide range of research investigators, and to trust science and its findings, even if these do not fit the government narrative, for the larger interest of the society. It is possible that many people are dying due to flawed science policies, lack of transparency about sharing key data, together with government officials' unwillingness to embrace the evidence-based truths from informed analyses by the scientists, and act proactively on them. By witnessing the gigantic achievements of India's scientific endeavor, with increased involvement of all sections of the society with abundant and renewed enthusiasm, along with trust, at the time of worst crisis in the human civilization, one can hope that India's spending on R&D that is now 0.8 per cent of GDP (Gross Domestic Product) as compared to 3 per cent in the USA, will increase substantially over time for the equitable, and sustainable benefits of the Indian society.

Figure 39. Comparison of India's cumulative confirmed deaths against fully vaccinated population.

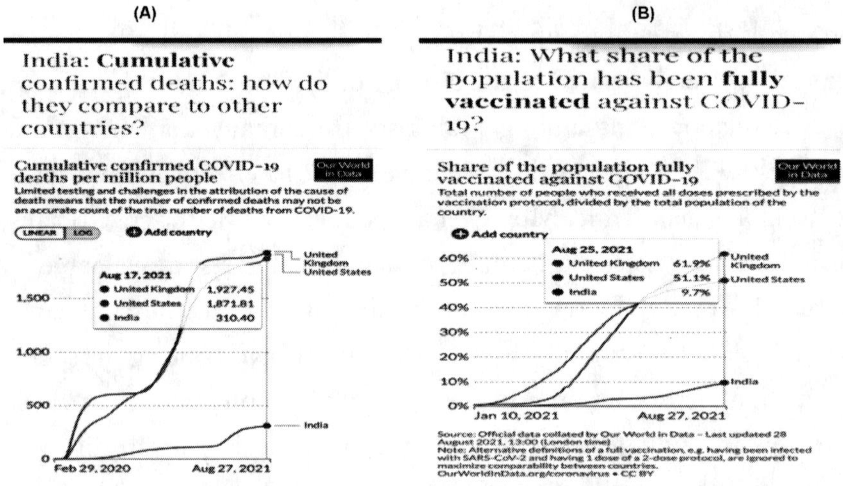

Source: Our World in Data.

References

India's COVID-19 response: science first. N. Radhakrishnan and D.K. Gupta. *The Lancet.* Vol. 397, Issue 10293, P2464-2465, June 26, 2021. DOI: https://doi.org/10.1016/S0140-6736(21)01241-1

Handbook for COVID-19 testing in Research Institutions. https://psa.gov.in/information-related-covid-19/handbook-covid-testing-research-laboratories

ICMR COVID-19 Analytics Portal. https://cvanalytics.icmr.org.in

CoviHawkes: An AI tool for district-wise forecasting and monitoring of COVID-19 infections in India. https://sml.csa.iisc.ac.in/covihawkes/

Covid-19 Sample Collection Management System for Rapid Antigen, Antibody and RT-PCR Tests. https://covid19cc.nic.in/ICMR/Login.aspx

COVID BEEP is India's first indigenous, cost effective, wireless physiological parameters monitoring system for COVID-19 patients. https://pib.gov.in/PressReleaseDetailm.aspx?PRID=1739880

Research on Ayush medicine system for treatment of Covid-19. https://pib.gov.in/PressRelaeaseDetailm.aspx?PRID=1741914

Scientists from four BRICS countries to carry out genome sequencing and mathematical modeling of the COVID-19 pandemic. https://dst.gov.in/scientists-four-brics-countries-carry-out-genomic-sequencing-and-mathematical-modelling-covid-19

India in Global Science: Bilateral Cooperation. https://www.indiascienceandtechnology.gov.in/bilateralcooperations?category=department-of-biotechnology

Year End Review-2020: DST, M/o Science & Technology. https://pib.gov.in/PressReleaseDetail.aspx?PRID=1689593

India's new science policy to be informed by COVID-19 crisis. DOI: https://doi.org/10.1038/nindia.2020.93. https://www.natureasia.com/en/nindia/article/10.1038/nindia.2020.93

Building a Science Diplomacy Curriculum. Jean-Christophe Mauduit and M. G. Soler. *Front. Edu.* 11 August 2020. DOI: https://doi.org/10.3389/feduc.20.20.00138).

Science Diplomacy A New Chapter in IISF2020, January-March 2021, Vol. 4(3), ISSN: 2456-5318.

Fighting COVID-19 viral variants with a heat-tolerant vaccine. https://www.iisc.ac.in/fighting-covid-19-viral-variants-with-a-heat-tolerant-vaccine/

C-CAMP Blackfrog Technologies gets H. T. Parekh Foundation's support to deliver vaccines in North East India. https://www.psa.gov.in/psa-prod/psa_custom_files/CCAMP-HTParekh-cold%20chain%20supply.pdf

Can coronavirus crisis change Indian science for good? https://m.economictimes.com/news/science/can-coronavirus-crisis-change-indian-science-for-good/articleshow/75224904.cms

TDB supported science-based startups play critical role in combating COVID 19. https://dst.gov.in/tdb-supported-science-based-startups-play-critical-role-combating-covid-19

Rethinking approcahes of science, technology, and innovation in healthcare during the COVID-19 pandemic: the challenge of translating knowledge infrastructures to public needs. R. G. Leonel de Silva, R. Charmas & H. M. Dutilh Novaes. *Health Research Policy and Systems* 19: 104(2021). DOI: https://doi.org/10.1186/s12961-021-00760-8

Indian government should heed its scientists on COVID. T.V. Padma. https://www.nature.com/articles/d41586-021-01140-6

IndiaFightsCorona COVID-19-MyGov. https://www.mygov.in/covid-19

Towards a Better Normal: A Global Perspective

"This is evolving science. You are seeing sausages being made-in front of the world's eyes."

– Saad Omer

"See, [the coronavirus is a like] a flu, not a cancer. Humanity has faced greater challenges. After the Spanish flu, we had the roaring twenties in America. And remember that 'crisis' and 'opportunity' have the same symbol in Chinese."

– Rakesh Jhunjhunwala

"If you're not generating big social benefits, you're not solving a problem, you're license to make a lot of money isn't so robust."

– Cameron Hepburn

Since the beginning of the ongoing pandemic, COVID-19 has been reshaping STI, impacting the society to a great extent. Factors that play key roles in shaping the future of STI, such as intensity of R&D across various sectors, the enthusiasm in adopting modern digital tools and technologies, the transparency, inclusiveness, and spontaneity of advanced research and innovation ecosystems, along with outreach programs, become more prominent in expanding benefits of STI uniformly across the world. The contribution of STI at this time of worst crisis, such as pandemic, is not only key for facing current health challenges, but, also for supporting sustainable production efforts targeted at accelerated economic recovery after the pandemic.

The contributions of STI revolutionize four major key areas: First, R&D to understand a new infectious disease, and its effects on the population and subsequent pharmacological intervention of the disease that includes vaccines, and other medications; second, management of critical supplies and equipments, such as diagnostic tests, mechanical ventilators, and the development of advanced applications for tracking and prevention of the infectious disease; third, economic recovery by developing digital platforms for health, education, work from home (WFH) and anywhere, smooth technology transfer for larger benefits, such as industrial reconversion and restructuring. Also, STI can effectively reduce a high socio-economic cost as a result of lowering the duration of hospitalization stay and associated treatment cost of COVID-19 victims through vaccinations, eliminating and/or reducing extensive lockdowns, and related sanitary and social distancing measures. Thus, it is critical to discuss and showcase the multiple benefits of STI that reshape the lives of the humans, and the society during the worst crisis from a global pandemic in the 21st century.

A rapid and renewed interest in collaborative research has emerged in the ongoing pandemic among universities, public research institutes, and pharmaceutical, and biotechnology firms across the world to quickly develop new effective treatment modalities and vaccines for COVID-19. The progress on vaccine development has been made in unprecedented way since the beginning of the pandemic. Several trackers provide real-time information on vaccine development that includes New York Times coronavirus vaccine tracker based on W.H.O. data. Interestingly, by mid-October 2020, the National

Institute of Health's (NIH) database in the USA listed more than 3,600 clinical trials on COVID-19 that had been conducted or were still under way around the world. The vast majority of ongoing clinical trails are targeted at interventional compounds to treat COVID-19.

The active and spontaneous engagement of the scientific community is reflected in the explosion of knowledge on the new disease in terms of scientific publications related to COVID-19. For example, by mid-April 2020, more than 3,500 articles had been published in the peer-reviewed journals that is way higher than the previous pandemics, according to PubMed, a free database supporting the search and retrieval of biomedical science literatures, managed by the US National Center for Biotechnology Information. Also, other major evidence for active intellectual engagement of the scientific community with the disease comes from an international survey of researchers in various disciplines, conducted by Springer Nature and Digital Science, during the period from 24 May to 18 June 2020, had found that 43 per cent of the 3,436 research investigators surveyed had existing or were likely to repurpose, and resubmit their grants for funding in COVID-19 research. The maps that show the country of origin of COVID-19 research clearly indicate that the USA and the People's Republic of China are among the major shareholders of COVID-19 publications on PubMed. Other countries with high engagements of international research efforts, include United Kingdom, Germany, France, Italy, Australia, Canada, and India.

Furthermore, a major impact of COVID-19 has been on the greater speed in disseminating the scientific findings in the society, by honoring the principle of open science. Many journals have increased the scope for fast-track publication, by accelerating the peer-review processes. A comparison of 669 articles published in 14 peer-reviewed medical journals, during and prior to the ongoing pandemic, finds that the downtime to publish a research article had significantly decreased by 49 per cent on average, from 117 days to 60 days. Also, OECD analysis of PubMed finds that the share of open-access research on COVID-19 was 76 per cent as opposed to 43 per cent for diabetes, and 40 per cent for dementia research, over the same period.

During the lockdown period, research and innovation activities requiring physical access to laboratories to conduct experiments, and other facilities were strongly disrupted. Therefore, researchers shifted to research activities that can be done from home, such as analyzing data, focused writing, publishing, and planning for future research that also resulted publication of larger proportion of research articles. Importantly, others invested their time and expertise to fight the COVID-19, by repurposing their research facilities, and equipments to serve COVID-related work. For example, the Francis Crick Institute in London, a cancer research center, has partly turned into a COVID-19 testing facility. This "COVID-isation" of research further boosted the collective effort in developing new knowledge to mitigate the deleterious effects of a new virus.

Moreover, apart from academic research, industry has moved to respond effectively to COVID-19 challenges. A survey showed that about 25 per cent of companies had repurposed their innovations in markets, such as communications, Internet services, sanitation and hospital services, even if this was not their primary industry.

A worldwide survey and subsequent interviews of more than 200 executives across various industries, conducted by McKinsey in April 2020, found that focus in innovation as a core business priority had increased in the pharmaceutical and medical supply sectors. Also, a large number of executives believed that changes brought about by COVID-19 would be an enormous opportunity for growth across diverse industries.

The ongoing COVID-19 pandemic has also resulted a boost in the successful adoption of digital substitutes. Severe restriction to travel imposed by the lockdown measures, compelled many of the conferences and events organized digitally with very attendance. These digital conferences are advantageous in terms of improved accessibility, reaching more diverse audience across the world, lower costs, and significant reduction in the carbon footprint of travel.

Furthermore, most nations have also implemented measures to boost rapid innovative responses, to a diverse range of challenges posed by COVID-19. For example, fast-track open competition was launched in the United kingdom to stimulate out-of-the-box thinking with inputs from researchers and inventors from all parts of the STI system, where applicants demonstrate the relevance of the their COVID-19- related work for funding. Also, virtual hackathons that are typically 24- to 48-hour events, were initiated that allowed the participants to share compelling pilot data to create an innovative product. Winners are compensated with funding to develop and scale their ideas.

In addition, there has been a tremendous boost in supporting data and knowledge sharing, such as epidemiological, clinical, and genomics data and studies among researchers across the world. The COVID-19 Open Research Database CORD-19, produced by the Allen Institute for artificial intelligence (AI) in partnership with US government and several firms, foundations and publishers, contains over 20,000 machine-readable scholarly articles on coronaviruses that serves as a basis for applying machine learning techniques to quickly generate novel insights to reducing the duplication of research efforts by other investigators for rapid advancement of COVID-19-related research. In addition, other initiatives include repositories of genomic data run by Nextstrain and Gisaid (Global initiative on sharing all influenza data) (www.gisaid.org), chemical-structure data, such as CAS COVID-19 data set on antiviral candidate compounds, ClinicalTrials.org that lists many of the ongoing clinical trials around the world, and data for modeling research, such as MIDAS (Molecular Interactive Data Acquisition System). Regulatory flexibility has also been introduced to ensure rapid health care responses to COVID-19 that involves expedited scientific advice and fast reviews of clinical-trial applications, and expedited clinical investigations of medical devices. Also, a significant boost in the research infrastructures, such as database and tools have been introduced to help researchers worldwide to improve research productivity over a short period of time. For example, the public-private COVID-19 High Performance Computing Consortium in the United States supports COVID-19 investigators across the world with access to high-performance computing.

Moreover, to address COVID-19 pandemic, program that accelerates the patent review process submitted by the small and micro entities, has been introduced without any extra cost for fast-track reviewing of the patent applications by The United States Patent and Trademark Office (USPTO).

The effects of COVID-19 have significant impact on technology sectors. From a positive perspective, the pandemic has resulted an acceleration of remote working, and a key focus on evaluating and de-risking the end-to-end value chain. In the technology sub-sectors, such as hardware and software industry, companies with remote-working technologies are witnessing increased demand and more revenues, as most of the businesses increase their remote-working facilities. Security software saw a potential benefits from a growing remote workforce. In addition, IT (Information Technology) spending on security software will expect to see a boost as organizations inclined to secure endpoints, especially cloud-based tools, log management, and VPNs (Virtual Private Network). Also, hardware companies may see a larger demand coming from enterprises, who are placing bulk orders for laptops and mobility services to support employees working from home and/ or anywhere. IT spending forecasts indicate continued demand for cloud infrastructure services, and increased spending on specialized software. Due to enhanced remote work activities, IT departments will play a key role in future BCPs (business-continuity plan). Thus, they need help from IT service providers in procuring devices, setting up an efficient network, and disaster recovery system along with security. Also, speeding up 5G network deployments, and adoption of 5G equipments are important for faster access to data and automation. This will further boost the semiconductor industry, the products of which are typically used in wired communication applications, and also in 5G communications. Increase in the use of teleconferencing software and network equipment, as a larger number of companies encourage employees to telecommunicate, will benefit companies that deal with these devices. Digitalization of diagnostics, development of advanced applications for effective tracking, and prevention of the COVID-19 disease have resulted a noticeable increase in the average share of products and/or services that are partially or fully digitalized across the different continents in the world. Also, COVID-19 pandemic has accelerated the digitalization of customer interactions. The year 2020 brought about several digital technologies that can be applied to tackle major clinical problems and diseases. For example, internet of things (IoT) with next-generation telecommunication network, blockchain technology, big-data analytics etc. are highly interrelated, that allow establishment of an interconnected digital ecosystem in hospital and clinics, enabling real-time data collection at scale, that could be used by AI (Artificial

Intelligence) and deep learning systems to better assess healthcare needs, facilitates further innovation, model risk assessment, such as possible emergence of infection outbreak, and effective strategy design based on predicted outcomes. This is enhanced by blockchain technology; highly efficient back-linked database with high security that uses cryptographic protocols and a network of distributed computers in different organizations. Moreover, it integrates peer-to-peer networks to ensure that data are copied in multiple physical locations, with modified algorithms to establish data security and traceability. Thus, essentially, they improve two major public-health strategies for handling COVID-19 crises, such as monitoring, surveillance, detection and prevention of COVID-19 and mitigating COVID-19-related impacts to healthcare system indirectly related to COVID-19.

The 'Worldmeter', a platform that uses IoT, provides a real-time update on the actual number of COVID-19 cases worldwide that includes daily new cases of the disease, its distribution across different countries, and severity of disease (recovered, critical condition or death). Also, Center for System Science and Engineering of John Hopkins University has developed a real-time tracking system for monitoring COVID-19 cases across the world, by integrating data source from US CDC, W.H.O, the European Center for Disease Prevention and Control, the Chinese Center for Disease Control and Prevention (China CDC) and the Chinese national website DXY; a data aggregator from China's National Health Commission and China CDC (Chinese Center for Disease Control and Prevention).

Furthermore, AI and deep learning also help to improve the detection and diagnosis of COVID-19. It is important to have low-cost tests for diagnosis of COVID-19 during the ongoing pandemic. Many peripheral hospitals in the developing, and underdeveloped countries have the tests or resource to accurately distinguish COVID-19 from the common flu. AI algorithm can be used as an initial screening tool for suspected cases, based on travel history so that patients at higher risk could have confirmatory laboratory-based tests or be isolated. China has large datasets for deep AI and deep learning that has more than 70,000 COVID-19 positive cases that can be used to train machine to distinguish confirmed COVID-19 cases from suspected cases. Also, AI can facilitate the discovery of new drugs or repurposing of the existing drugs to treat COVID-19 disease.

Healthcare system can be revolutionized using digital technologies by mitigating the impact of an infectious disease, such as COVID-19. For example, virtual clinics could be set up through the use of telemedicine consultations with imaging data, such as chest X-ray and/or CT of the thorax, uploaded from peripheral sites, and interpreted at a remote location, that allows patients to receiving standard clinical care while reducing crowding at the hospital premises. Also, many emergency meetings are increasingly being done with the help of virtual e-learning platforms to eliminate physical meetings. Phone-based software and smart watches that detect and record patients' data, such as daily temperature and symptoms might alleviate the volume of unnecessary in-person consultations for patients with mild flu-like symptoms. Importantly, the stored data can be correlated with the actual COVID-19 disease symptoms clinically, and subsequently can be further utilized to train a new algorithm for fast-track detection of COVID-19 disease. Additionally, many hospitals in China are building key collaborations with blockchain companies and pharmacies for timely delivery of patients' medication to their doorsteps. Blockchain technology helps timely delivery of medications with accurate tracking. Thus, an explosive development of blockchain technologies aimed at targeted disease, such as COVID-19 has emerged during the ongoing pandemic.

Taken together, the rapid progress of STI during the ongoing COVID-19 pandemic, will support the three dimensions to managing a crisis: respond, recover, and thrive. It is important to continuously drive science, technology and innovation, and their adoptions to support the future of scenarios, and ameliorate the asymmetric impacts of the COVID-19 crisis across sectors, countries, and among various states in a country. However, there are still many unknowns that need to be addressed as we move along the pandemic. How long will the various vaccines made worldwide, protect us from getting new infections? How will the virus mutate resulting more new variants? Is it possible to reach the herd immunity, and when? And finally, when the world will see an end to this never-ending pandemic? Nevertheless, as the saying goes, 'a crisis provides an opportunity'; this unprecedented crisis of 2020-2021 gives global society a great opportunity to understand better the importance of STI, and how we can safeguard the society, through new scientific discoveries, inventing, and adopting newer technologies to respond adequately against any infectious and/or non-infectious life-threatening diseases, leading to a better normal than before, and further improve the quality-adjusted life years (QALYS) of the global population.

Figure 40. International scientific collaboration on COVID-19: **(A)** A map with four clusters (communities), was created based on economy affiliation bibliographic data. Economies are assigned to clusters based on their interconnection. The color of an item is determined by the cluster to which it belongs. The higher the weight of an item, the larger its label and circle. Lines between items represents links. In general, the closer two economies are located to each other, the stronger is relatedness. The strongest co-authorship links between economies are also represented by lines. The whole counts were till 30 November 2020 from January 2020 **(B),** international COVID research collaborations as a percentage of papers between January 2020 and December 2020 **(C),** citation advantage of published research articles among various countries as a result of collaborations.

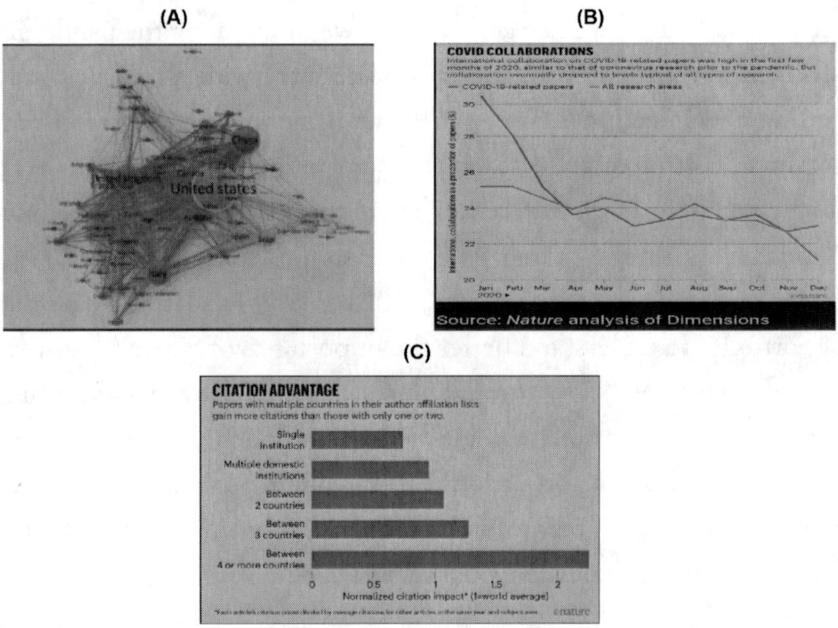

Source: OECD and OCTS-OEI calculations, based on NIH PubMed data, https://doi.org/10.1787/888934223099. OCED=The Organization for Economic Co-operation and Development, OCTS-OEI=The Observatory for Science, technology and Innovation of the Organization of Ibero-American States; Nature analysis of Dimensions, *Nature*.

Figure 41. Innovation and growth in various industries across diverse sectors during COVID-19 pandemic:

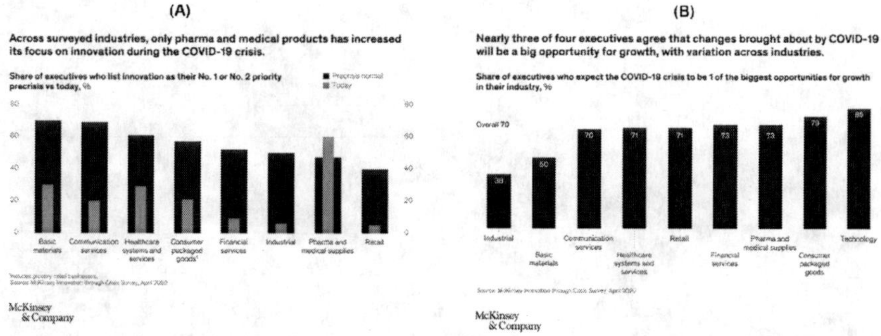

Source: McKinsey & Company.

Figure 42. Digital technologies and their impacts on **(A),** public-health strategies **(B),** customer interactions **(C),** products and services, and **(D),** miscellaneous sectors.

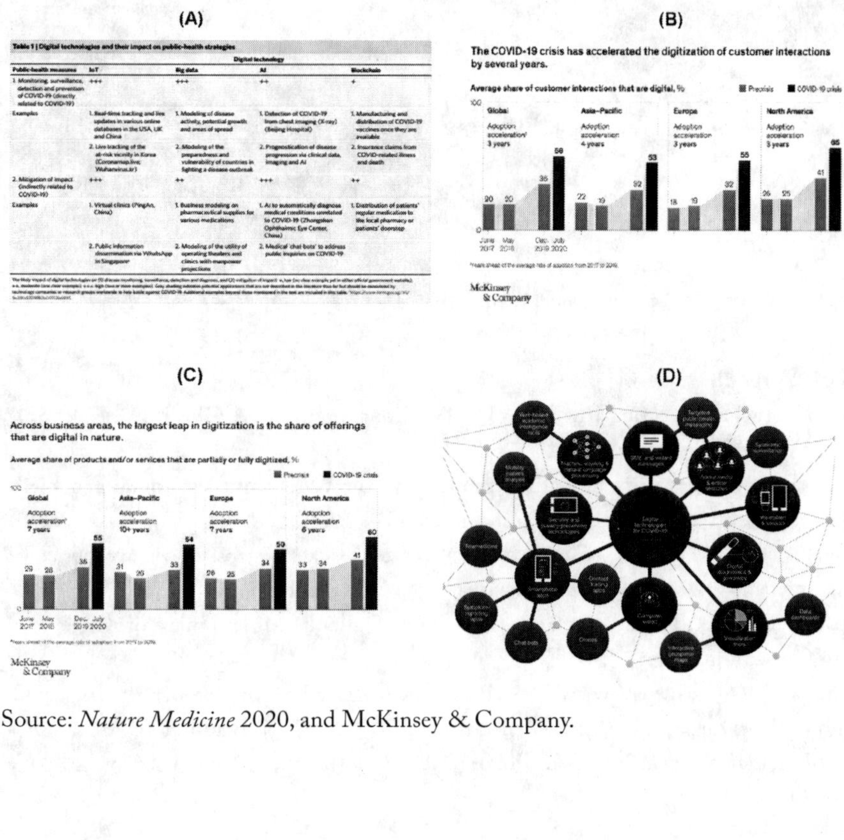

Source: *Nature Medicine* 2020, and McKinsey & Company.

Figure 43. The contributions of immunological societies to the global response to the COVID-19 pandemic.

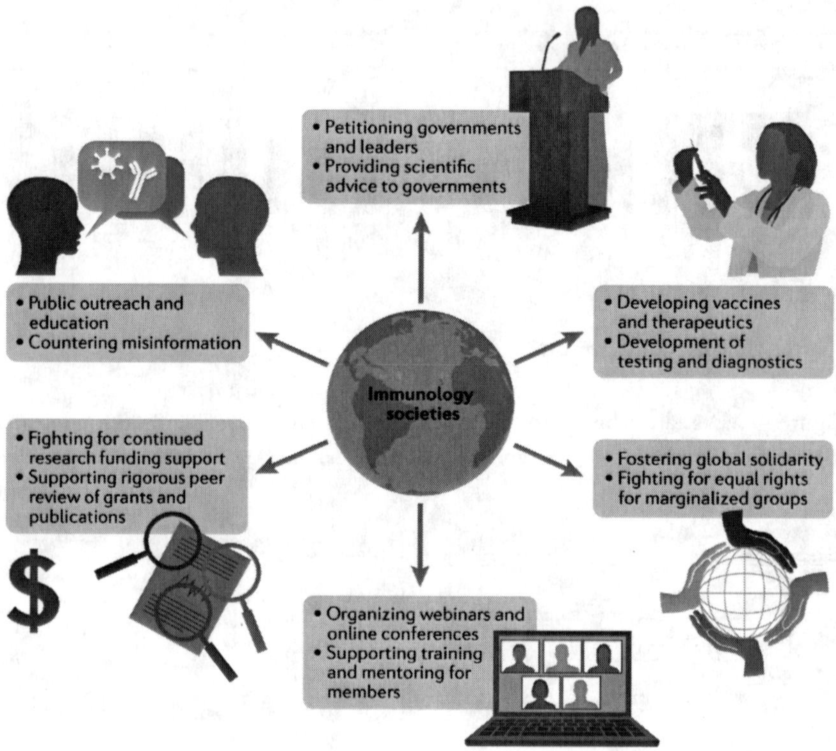

Source: *Nature Review Immunology*, 2020.

References

OECD: Tackling Coronavirus (COVID-19): Contributing to A Global Effort. https://www.oecd.org/coronavirus

COVID-19 Observatory in Latin America and the Caribbean: Economic and social impact. https://www.cepal.org/en/topics/covid-19.

The New York Times: Coronavirus Vaccine Tracker. https://www.nytimes.com/interactive/2020/science/coronavirus-vaccine-tracker.html

OECD Science, Technology and Innovation Outlook 2021: Times of Crisis and Opportunity

ClinicalTrials.gov, https://www.clinicaltrials.gov (accessed on 16 October 2020).

"Innovation During a Crisis: Evidence from COVID-19", K. Bryan et al. 2020. *SSRN Electronic Journal*, https://dx.doi.org/10.2139/ssrn.3587973 (accessed on 20 May 2020).

G. Baynes and M. Hahnel, 2020. "Research Practices in the Wake of COVID-19: Busting open the myths around open data", *Springer Nature,* https://www.springernature.com/gp/advancing-discovery/blog/blogposts/research-practices-in-the-wake-of-covid/18256280 (accessed on 28 September 2020).

S. Horbach, 2020. *Pandemic Publishing: Medical journals drastically speed up their publication process for Covid-19,* Cold Spring Harbor Laboratory, https://dx.doi.org/10.1101/2020.04.18.045963).

How the COVID pandemic is changing global science collaborations. R. Maher and R. V. Noorden. *Nature* 594, 316-319 (2021). DOI: https://doi.org/10.1038/d41586-021-01570-2.

Tens of thousands of scientists are redeploying to fight coronavirus. *Nature*, 27 March 2020. DOI: https://doi.org/10.1038/d41586-020-00905-9

N. Baker, 2020. These cancer scientists turned their lab into a coronavirus-testing facility. G. Viglione, 2020. *Nature.* 580, 441 (2020). DOI: https://doi.org/10.1038/d41586-020-01109-x

V. Kanesarajah and E. White (2020). Chasing change: Innovation and potent activity during COVID-19. A report on the pandemic's impact on the global R&D community and innovation lifecycle, *Clarivate,* https://clarivate.com/derwent/blog/chasing-change-innovation-and-patent-activity-during-covid-19).

https://www.semanticscholar.org/cord19

https://www.cas.org/covid-19-antiviral-compounds-dataset

https://midasnetwork.us/covid-19/

Science in the time of COVID 19. Editorial. *Nat Hum Behav* 4, 327-328 (2020). DOI: https://doi.org/10.1038/s41562-020-0879-9.

The global response to the COVID-19 pandemic: how have immunology societies contributed? F. Osier et al. *Nature Reviews Immunology* 20, 594-602 (2020). DOI: https://doi.org/10.1038/s41577-020-00428-4.

https://www.gov.uk/guidance/mhra-regulatory-flexibilities-resulting-from-coronavirus-covid-19).

https://www.whitehouse.gov/briefings-statements/white-house-announces-new-partnership-unleash-u-s-supercomputing-resources-fight-covid-19/).

https://www.uspto.gov/about-us/news-updates/uspto-announces-covid-19-prioratized-examination-pilot-program-small-and-micro-entities) (accessed on 25 May 2020).

Deloitte: Understanding the sector impact of COVID-19-Technology sector.

Digital technologies in the public-health response to COVID-19. J. Budd et al. *Nature Medicine* 26, 1183-1192 (2020). DOI: https://doi.org/10.1038/s41591-020-1011-4.

The Internet of Things comes to the lab. J.M. Perkel. *Nature* 542, 125-126 (2017). DOI: https://doi.org/10.1038/542125a

Artificial intelligence, the internet of things, and virtual clinics: ophthalmology at the digital translation forefront. D.S.W. Ting et al. *Lancet Digital Health* Vol. 2, Issue 1, E8-E9, January 01, 2020. DOI: https://doi.org/10.1016/S2589-7500(19)30217-1

Bitcoin for the biological literature. D. Heaven. *Nature* 566, 141-142 (2019). DOI: https://doi.org/10.1038/d41586-019-00447-9

Digital technology and COVID-19. D.S.W. Ting et al. *Nat Med* 26, 459-461 (2020). DOI: https://doi.org/10.1038/s41591-020-0824-5).

https://www.worldmeters.info/coronavirus/

https://gisanddata.maps.arcgis.com/apps/opsdashboard/index.htlm#/bda7594740fd40299423467b48e9eef6).

https://www.wired.com/story/chinese-hospitals-deploy-ai-help-diagnosis-covid-19

https://www.vox.com/recode/2020/2/27/21156358/surveillance-tech-coronavirus-china-facial-recognition

Conclusion

The ongoing COVID-19 pandemic has been devastating in the world, with cumulative confirmed cases of more than 2.5 billion, including about 50 million deaths, reported to W.H.O., as of 10 November, 2021.

Over the entire 2020, non-pharmacological interventions (NPI) have been the only modalities, to control the transmission of SARS-CoV-2 infections, from human-to-human, when researchers worldwide, trying to develop effective vaccines against COVID-19, as NPI are not full-proof modalities, against the deadly COVID-19 disease.

However, the world needs to boost its economic recovery quickly, after a devastating spell of economic downturn in 2020, as a result of lockdowns and stringent retractions on business activities, to keep the infections levels down in the society. Thus, pharmacological intervention, such as effective vaccines against COVID-19 disease, along with NPI, is essential to reinitiate the economic activities in 2021, similar to the pre-pandemic period.

Interestingly, recent data on the real-world effectiveness of some newly developed vaccines against COVID-19 have shown significant progress in controlling the disease transmission, severity of the disease, and the death rates in the population.

Although, the worldwide vaccination rate has been encouraging, a significant fraction of the population is still skeptical about the effectiveness, and safety of the newly developed COVID-19 vaccines. Since, it is a new infectious disease, misinformation about the disease trajectory, quick evolving knowledge about the nature of new virus, and its evolving variants, has compelled general population, to embrace misinformation about vaccines, spearheaded by anti-science communities around the world, resulting vaccine hesitancy in the general population.

Thus, the COVID-19 pandemic has brought Science & Technology, and Innovation (STI), scientists, entrepreneurs, policy makers to the forefront of public engagements and scrutiny. A stellar performance in managing the deadly disease, by inventing technology-driven tracking and testing of the SARS-CoV-2, and its variants, and predicting the disease outbreak, that will strengthen the pandemic preparedness in the society, and build the scientific mindset of the general population, by disseminating true scientific information about the virus, new developments in the STI sector, and the vaccines, is the key to win trust in the society.

Since the beginning of the ongoing pandemic, COVID-19 has been reshaping STI, science and social policy, such as vaccine equity and Sustainable Development Growths (SDGs), impacting the society to a great extent. Additionally, the explosive information about the scientific and technological developments, and its periodic updates, during the worst crisis of the 21st century, need to be put together in the form of a book, to enlighten the society, about its importance in reshaping their lives, and to establish a social blueprint, driven by the STI, for sustainable bright future of the society.

Taken together, it is indeed important to showcase the rapid progress of STI, during the ongoing COVID-19 pandemic that captures the three dimensions to managing a crisis: respond-understanding the new disease, recover- development of vaccines and other treatment modalities, and thrive-innovative modern technology, and its implementation. Thus, the book entitled "Convergence of

Science and Society: Pandemic 2020" intends to disseminate the key information to its readers, about STI including vaccine development and its progress, in response to worldwide COVID-19 pandemic.

The pathway from vaccine development to the vaccination is long, and many steps are involved throughout the entire process. Previously, many vaccines were made in combating a multitude of infectious diseases, other than COVID-19 around the world. Thus, the history of vaccines is indeed rich, in terms of knowledge, and their usefulness. Moreover, a thorough fundamental understanding of the biology of immunity in humans, mediated either naturally or through vaccines, is important for the readers, to better understand the intricacies of vaccine developments, and its effectiveness. The various technology platforms that are typically used for vaccine development are extensively discussed in the book. Also, the fundamental underlying mechanism(s) by which vaccines work in the population are incorporated in this book. The real-world effectiveness of the newly developed COVID-19 vaccines, that are currently being used to combat disease spread worldwide, is discussed in one of the sections of the book. The temporal emergence of COVID-19 variants, and their immune escape mechanisms are included in the book, as well. Importantly, the detailed information on vaccination drive in India, which is one of the worst affected countries, in this ongoing pandemic, is discussed in the book. The health, social, and economic benefits of vaccination, social policy, such as vaccine equity, and SDGs are included in the book. All of the relevant information is incorporated in appropriate separate section in the part one of the book 'The Tell Tale of Vaccination'.

The part two of this book 'The Multifaceted Societal Impact of COVID-19 on Science & Technology, and Innovation: Indian and Global Perspective', captures the gigantic new developments, and progress of STI, its policy in response to COVID-19 disease worldwide. It discusses the innovative technological development, such as digitalization of diagnostics, establishment of virtual clinics, contactless emergency health advice, and monitoring of the COVID-19 victims, that gives a new dimension to the existing healthcare system, for the larger benefits of the society, especially, in a crisis situation. Additionally, this part of the book, discusses the explosive development in the scientific publishing, and fast-track research funding opportunities to bring COVID-19-related discoveries rapidly to the society around the world. Essentially, the part two of the new book, captures the key information about STI that are helpful in managing a worst crisis, in terms of response, recovery, and thrive, against the deadly COVID-19 disease.